Better Homes and Gardens®

Decks

Meredith® Books
Des Moines, Iowa

Table of contents

PLANNING A DECK

TOOLS, MATERIALS, AND TECHNIQUES

BUILDING A BASIC DECK

FRAMING VARIATIONS

Deck Variations

Deck Features

Finishes, Maintenance, and Repairs

Better Homes and Gardens® Decks
Editor: Larry Johnston
Copy Chief: Terri Fredrickson
Copy Editor: Kevin Cox
Publishing Operations Manager: Karen Schirm
Senior Editor, Asset and Information Management: Phillip Morgan
Edit and Design Production Coordinator: Mary Lee Gavin
Art and Editorial Sourcing Coordinator: Jackie Swartz
Editorial Assistant: Kaye Chabot
Book Production Managers: Pam Kvitne, Marjorie J. Schenkelberg, Mark Weaver
Imaging Center Operator: Ben Anderson
Contributing Copy Editors: Don Gulbrandsen, Cheri Madison
Contributing Proofreaders: Carolyn Hogan, David Krause, Willa Speiser
Contributing Technical Proofreader: Barbara L. Klein
Contributing Indexer: Don Glassman
Other Contributors: Janet Anderson

Additional Editorial Contributions from Abramowitz Creative Studios
Publishing Director/Designer: Tim Abramowitz
Designer/Illustrator: Kelly Bailey
Designer: Joel Wires
Photography: Image Studios
    Account Executive: Lisa Egan
    Photographer: Bill Rein
    Assistant: Rick Nadke

Meredith® Books
Editor in Chief: Gregory H. Kayko
Executive Director, Design: Matt Strelecki
Managing Editor: Amy Tincher-Durik
Executive Editor/Group Manager: Benjamin W. Allen
Senior Associate Design Director: Tom Wegner
Marketing Product Manager: Brent Wiersma

Executive Director, Marketing and New Business: Kevin Kacere
Director, Marketing and Publicity: Amy Nichols
Executive Director, Sales: Ken Zagor
Director, Operations: George A. Susral
Director, Production: Douglas M. Johnston
Business Director: Janice Croat

Senior Vice President: Karla Jeffries
Vice President and General Manager: Douglas J. Guendel

Meredith Publishing Group
President: Jack Griffin
Executive Vice President: Doug Olson

Meredith Corporation
Chairman of the Board: William T. Kerr
President and Chief Executive Officer: Stephen M. Lacy

In Memoriam: E.T. Meredith III (1933–2003)

All of us at Meredith® Books are dedicated to providing you with the information and ideas you need to enhance your home and garden. We welcome your comments and suggestions. Write to us at:
Meredith Books
Home Improvement Books Department
1716 Locust St.
Des Moines, IA 50309–3023

Note to the Readers: Due to differing conditions, tools, and individual skills, Meredith Corporation assumes no responsibility for any damages, injuries suffered, or losses incurred as a result of following the information published in this book. Before beginning any project, review the instructions carefully, and if any doubts or questions remain, consult local experts or authorities. Because codes and regulations vary greatly, you always should check with authorities to ensure that your project complies with all applicable local codes and regulations. Always read and observe all of the safety precautions provided by manufacturers of any tools, equipment, or supplies, and follow all accepted safety procedures.

PLANNING A DECK

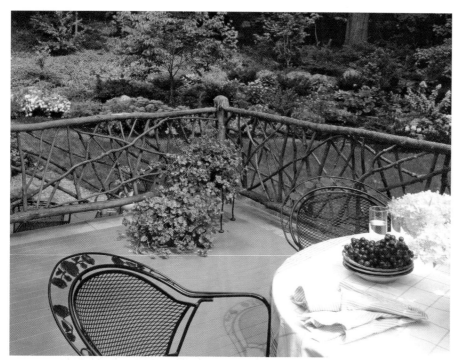

Put in some personality

Railings provide an opportunity to customize a deck. This railing, assembled from rustic rails and branches, complies with local building codes. Check with your building inspector before installing any railing.

Accessorize for beauty

Furniture and accessories make a deck comfortable and inviting. Containers with plants add color and lend softness to the hard surfaces of a deck. Flower beds help blend the deck into the landscape. Wicker furniture enhances the casual look, and curtains hung on a track provide movable shade and privacy screening.

Terminology

A deck is an outdoor floor supported by posts and footings in the ground. The following terms define the components of a typical deck. Specific types of decks may differ.

Beams or girders: Hefty framing members (usually 4×, 6×, or doubled 2× stock) attached horizontally to the posts to support the joists.

Decking: 2× or 5/4 stock attached to the joists to form the floor of the deck.

Footings: Concrete columns below grade that support the posts and, thus, the deck. On sites where the soil freezes and thaws, concrete is poured in a form inserted in a hole that's dug to frost depth. Ask your building department for footing depths in your area.

Headers: Framing members perpendicular to the joists and attached to their ends.

Joists: Horizontal framing members (usually 2× stock) fastened on top of the beam or flush with the ledger

to support the decking. A header is fastened to the ends of the deck's interior joists. Rim joists or end joists are the outermost joists perpendicular to the ledger.

Ledger: A header attached to the house to support one side of the deck.

Piers: (not illustrated) Precast concrete pyramids made to be set on inground footings or, where frost heave is not a factor, directly on the ground to support posts.

Post anchors: Metal framing connectors that attach posts to piers or footings. Some types raise the base of the posts slightly above the top of the footings, protecting them from water and insect damage.

Posts: Timbers (usually 4× or 6×) set vertically to support the deck framing. Posts are used on all but the shortest decks. The posts can be cut off below the deck surface, or they may rise above the surface to provide support for the railing. Posts may rest on top of

concrete footings, or they can be set in the hole before the concrete is poured.

Rails: Horizontal components of railings that provide a safety barrier and handhold for stairs or along the sides of the deck.

Railing: The assembly made of rails, rail posts, cap rails, and balusters or spindles. Balusters, the smallest vertical components, are positioned to fill the space between the top and bottom rails and between rail posts. Maximum baluster spacing for child safety is 4 inches.

Risers: Boards that enclose the vertical spaces between stairway treads. Risers are often omitted on deck steps and other exterior steps.

Stringers: Long diagonal framing members (usually 2×12s) that support stairs. The stair treads are attached to the stringers.

Treads: The horizontal stepping surfaces of a stairway.

Working to code

Local communities enact building codes to establish standards for safety, aesthetics, and durability. "Working to code" means knowing and understanding local building codes and complying with them as you build a project.

Many building codes consider a deck to be a permanent addition, so there are regulations that define footing depths, material choices, and fence heights. Check with your local building department before you start your project planning.

As a private individual working on a deck for your own use on your own property, you have the same responsibility to satisfy building authorities as a professional carpenter or contractor. Submit plans to your building department for approval and obtain a building permit. Depending on its policies the building department may also want to inspect your work periodically to make sure you're following the plans they approved. Failing to comply with codes could result in an order to remove what you've built.

Not everyone is required to get a building permit. It's up to you, not the authorities, to find out what laws cover your project.

Besides building codes you may find that the following issues can affect your deck design.

Zoning ordinances
These regulate the use of property and the placement of structures on it. They can establish minimum setbacks from property lines, easements, and the size of your deck. In recent years many communities have established limits on the amount of deck surface because large areas of hardscape increase the flow of runoff into storm sewers.

Deed restrictions
Some communities adopt deed restrictions to control property values or architectural style. These may restrict the style of your deck and the materials you can use.

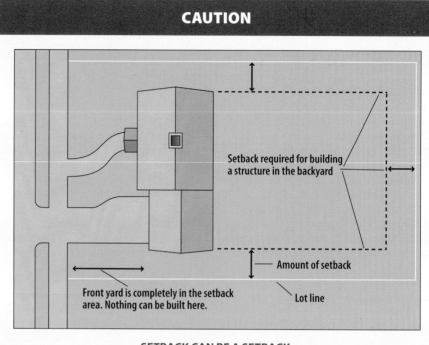

CAUTION

Setback required for building a structure in the backyard

Amount of setback

Front yard is completely in the setback area. Nothing can be built here.

Lot line

SETBACK CAN BE A SETBACK
You own the property inside your property lines but that doesn't mean you can build your deck next to the borders. Local building codes or zoning ordinances may require you to observe setback requirements—a specified distance from adjoining property lines. Check with local officials before drawing any plans.

Easements and rights of way
These rules guarantee access by utilities to their lines and may restrict your ability to build a deck where you want to. Before you get too far into your planning, contact the utility companies to flag the path of underground lines through your property. Most will do this for free and with one call to a central agency.

The procedures in this book will satisfy most local codes, but codes can vary widely—and they can change from time to time. Always check with your city or county building department.

Working with inspectors
To avoid unnecessary questions about your plans, obtain as much information as possible about local requirements and incorporate what you learn into your plan before you take it in for approval. Your building department may have publications that list requirements for the type of project you have planned.

Go to your building department with a plan to be approved; don't expect the inspectors to plan the job for you. Present your plan with neatly drawn diagrams and a complete list of the materials you will use.

Be sure you understand clearly at what stages of your project you need to have inspections. Do not cover up plumbing or electrical installations that need to be inspected.

Take time to do high-quality work. Inspectors often are wary of homeowners because so many do shoddy work. Show the inspector you are serious by following your approved plan and completing the work correctly.

Choosing a site

Where to build your deck may seem obvious at first, but take time to make sure the first site choice is really the best one. Slight changes in location or design may result in a more enjoyable deck.

The deck should relate to your home and landscape, including the architectural style of your house. The ideal location for your deck should allow easy access from indoors and out, make the best use of desirable views, hide undesirable ones, and provide enough privacy that you don't feel you're on display.

The site should also take advantage of sun and shade patterns, prevailing breezes, and other conditions to provide maximum comfort and usability.

Consider these factors before you commit to the final location for the deck. Look at your proposed site and list its assets and liabilities. Then use your notes to draw a site analysis. You may have to evaluate several options, but if you make those decisions early, you'll be more likely to build a deck that is enjoyable to use.

A well-designed deck should be visible from inside the house and easy to get to, and its purpose should be similar to the adjacent interior room. Interior designers call these factors access and compatibility. Taking them into account can help you design and build a deck useful and enjoyable deck.

Visual and physical access

When you can see your deck from inside the house, it invites you out to use it. If your proposed site can't be seen from inside the house, including new windows or doors in your plans might make it more suitable. You don't need to see the whole deck from inside the house; a glimpse is often more effective than a full view of the deck.

Make the view attractive from the inside. Geometric decking patterns, a decorative railing design, or container gardens are attractive visual enticements. And if you can see these attractions from more than one room, so much the better. If you can't, just design your deck space so the largest view is from the room that adjoins it.

Looking out at your deck isn't the only thing that matters, of course. You have to be able to get to it easily. To make sure the pathway to the deck is open and free of obstructions, make a sketch of the routes people use when walking through your home (below). If the proposed deck location would create traffic jams, make alterations. For example, although a deck next to your kitchen might seem ideal for outdoor dining, it may make the traffic in your cooking space unbearable. Moving a door to a sidewall could redirect the traffic away from the work areas.

Compatibility

The success of your deck may depend on its nearest indoor room. Most people use a deck more frequently if its use is similar to that of the interior room next to it. For example, a small deck for coffee or morning conversation would be just right outside your bedroom. But that would be the wrong place for a large party deck.

For outdoor dining put the deck close to the kitchen. Plan party or social areas close to the family room or other public rooms of the house. For private space, limit access to the deck and shield it from outside views with hedges or fencing.

LANDSCAPING YOUR DECK

Even a perfectly planned deck can look like an intrusion into your landscape. Thoughtful landscaping can make the deck seem more like a natural extension of the yard. A perennial border garden, for example, will ease the transition from the deck to the yard. Shrubs can hide the deck framing and gaping empty space beneath the surface. Baskets, pots, and planters will unify the entire area with color and texture.

Make access easy

If you can't go to and from your deck without bumping into obstructions, you probably won't use it. To make access easy, start with a wide doorway—French, atrium, or sliding glass doors permit easy in-and-out traffic and offer views that invite you outside. Add a door, if necessary, or widen an existing one. Analyze the natural pathways inside your house and place furniture to provide uninterrupted access from interior rooms to the deck.

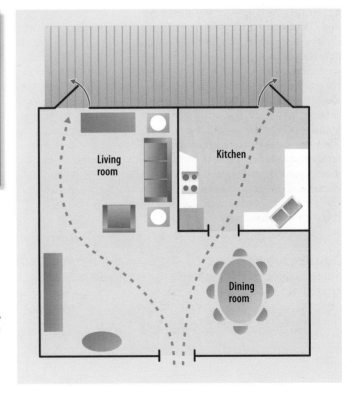

Site inventory

Before you make final plans, assess your property to see how the terrain and climate might affect the deck location.

Terrain is the characteristic that will probably affect your deck site the most. Deck construction is relatively straightforward on flat land. A slope might require grading, a retaining wall, or an elevated deck. A deck can make a hillside an opportunity instead of an obstacle. High slopes offer magnificent views. Land that slopes up from a deck site provides natural privacy and shelter from the wind.

Terrain can affect temperature too. A deck on a hill will feel warmer than one at the foot of an incline because cooler air flows downhill. If you trap that cool air with a retaining wall or a fence, your deck might feel cold after sunset.

Most people prefer a deck to be shaded for comfort, so track shade patterns by driving stakes in the yard. If your proposed site is naturally shaded, your decisions will be easier. If you need additional shade, you can make some. Trees and other plants can shade a site that gets too much afternoon sun. A pergola, especially one with a slatted roof to filter the sunlight, or an umbrella table are other possibilities for shade. Vines climbing up a lattice wall can cool off a site that gets hot in the late afternoon.

Note prevailing winds too. You may have to build or plant a windbreak to shelter a deck from strong winds. Be wary of solid fences; they create low-pressure pockets that pull the wind into the area you want protected. Louvers and lattice are good options—closed enough to add privacy but open enough to let some breezes through. You can't chart the rain, but you can protect yourself with solid roofing over a part of your deck. Or add an awning that you can retract when the skies are clear.

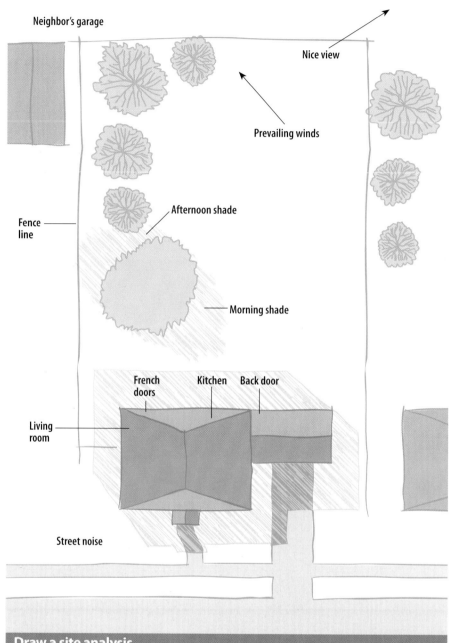

Draw a site analysis

Combine all your notes about your landscape in a site analysis. Start with a sketch of your yard and house, including the doors and windows, as well as utility hookups, walkways, bushes, and trees. Show views you want to keep and those you want to block out. Note the movement of the sun and where shade falls during different parts of the day. Add every detail that could affect the deck location—prevailing winds, septic tanks, utility lines, setbacks, and downspouts. When putting your deck plans on paper, lay tracing paper over the site analysis to sketch possible shapes and locations for the deck.

Determining deck size

Like many other questions about building a deck, deciding how large it should be probably will be easier once you've determined how you're going to use the deck. The chart below shows rough estimates of the space required for different activities. Use these as a guide to sizing your deck.

If your deck will have several uses (a play area for the kids, space for dining, an area for sunning), you may be tempted to make it as big as possible. But multiple functions don't always call for more deck; they may not all occur at the same time. Sometimes a design feature, such as a level change, can separate functional zones. Nonetheless, it's a good idea to use the high end of your size estimate for a single-level deck. Building more area is less costly than adding it later, and a cramped deck will disappoint you. If your budget is tight, plan a deck that you can build in stages and add to as you can afford to, keeping the overall design intact.

Cut down on mowing

A wraparound redwood deck with a wrought-iron railing transforms a narrow, unused side yard from lawn space into an open-air veranda. It's small but still has plenty of room for casual conversation. A deck like this can expand living area with style and will reduce mowing time.

TEST THE SITE SIZE

To test the size of your deck site, lay a rope or garden hose around the proposed area. Bring in the furniture, including the barbecue grill, lounge chairs, tables, and recliners.

Adjust the size until you're sure the deck will have room for all of your planned activities. Then step back and consider its scale.

A deck should be proportional to the house and grounds. If your deck is small, you probably won't have much of a scale problem, but large decks often look too big next to a modest home. Start with a design that fits the uses you envision, then scale back to fit the limits of your budget and terrain.

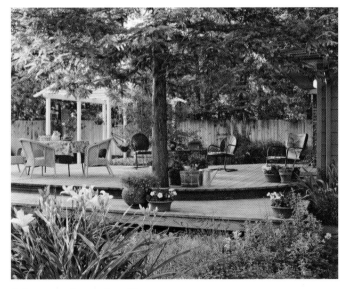

A breezy boardwalk

If you're designing a single-level deck large enough for small and large gatherings and want to dress the platform inexpensively, add a perimeter boardwalk. This narrow extension provides a little more room at a fraction of the cost of an additional platform. And guests will have a way to move to the far end of the deck without passing through the main activity sections. Movable furnishings define spaces casually.

HOW BIG?

Activity	Space required
Dining for 4 for 6 to 8	About 10×10 ft. 12×12 ft.
Conversation area for 6	About 10×10 ft.
Single reclining chair	About 4×7 ft.
Two recliners	About 7×7 ft.
Basic cooking area with grill	A space about 6 ft. square; more for counter, island, or large serving table
Rectangular table	An area 5 to 6 ft. wider and longer than the table itself
A round table for 6	Circular area, 9 ft. in diameter
Pathways, real and imaginary	$3\frac{1}{2}$ to 4 ft. wide at all points

Creating privacy

P rivacy will help you feel more comfortable and at home on your deck because you won't feel exposed.

Stand in each section of the deck site outlined on the ground (see page 11). Sit in all the chairs. Can your neighbors see your every move? Is your deck open to views from the sidewalk or street? Even if the neighbors' homes aren't close, do you feel unprotected and exposed? If so, you need more privacy.

Building a deck on an unexposed side of the house may solve the problem. But if your yard doesn't offer an architectural fix, add screening— a privacy fence, a wall, or trees and shrubs. You can apply different remedies to different parts of the deck.

Spaces planned for quiet or solitary activities, such as reading, conversation, sunbathing, or meditation, should be well screened. Screen pools and spas too. To enhance privacy you can build walls or fences or plant dense rows of evergreen shrubs.

Areas for large gatherings or children's play don't demand as much privacy. Partial screens—trees, latticework, picket fences, or low seat walls—are often adequate. Train vines onto a trellis—the leaves will ultimately hide the structure and make it seem as if nature created the privacy screen.

DON'T FENCE YOURSELF IN

Place screens strategically. Before you encircle your deck with shrubs or a solid fence, locate the spots where other people can see you. Block the most revealing views first. Strive to enhance your privacy without barricading yourself. Lattice, pickets, and ornamental iron fencing are more friendly because they don't block the view completely. The closer a screen is to the deck, the more privacy it adds.

Designing overhead structures

O verhead structures, such as pergolas and arbors, are usually made for shade. But that's not their only use; they also can enhance the aesthetics of the deck and complete the sense of enclosure.

Outdoor areas usually feel more comfortable with some kind of physical limit overhead, but it must be the right amount. A space intended for large groups can have a high overhead structure (or none at all). Smaller, private areas for dining, conversing, or relaxing will seem more inviting with a lower roof.

An arbor, pergola, canopy, or retractable awning can also protect you from the elements, especially harsh sunlight. Slats in a roof can cast shade on the deck. With careful attention to the spacing, orientation, and angle of the slats, you can control the amount of light that passes through.

No matter what kind of overhead structure you build, integrate it into the overall design. Incorporate some detail from your home into the design— a molding or post style, the pitch of the roof, an accent color, or building material. Linking the structure to your home can turn any deck into a unique addition to your landscape.

WHAT'S UP

Stand at various spots on your proposed deck site and look up. If you see open sky, you may need an overhead structure, even if you don't need the shade.

Tree branches 15 to 20 feet above the ground might be suitable cover for a large party area but could make an intimate table for two feel exposed. A table with an umbrella will make the site a bit cozier.

A cover 10 to 12 feet above the deck surface usually suits a small, private area. Shelter at least one-third of the surface area of your deck.

Designing for style

Questions about style often intimidate homeowners. But most people develop a sense of personal style as they decorate rooms inside the house. Designing an outdoor living space is little different from designing inside rooms.

Follow a theme when planning your deck. You can organize your deck along formal or informal lines or you can establish an Oriental, Southwestern, or Mediterranean theme. You can bring in the colors, textures, and culture of your area. Be cool, serene, and comfortable with a contemporary scheme that uses bold shapes and colors, sleek lines, and complementary geometric arrangements. Or forget about categories altogether and develop a style that incorporates eclectic elements that might even seem incongruous. They may fit perfectly on your deck.

Style is in the details, especially the railings, stairs, and the pattern of the decking. If your deck reflects your personality, you'll use it more often and enjoy it more.

Plant the edges
Put plantings at the edges of your deck. Carefully chosen containers can cover the edges of the structure and create a transition into the surrounding landscape.

Accent the railing
Railings are the most visible element of a deck and make an instant design statement. Add appeal by including accents in your railing design. A corniced panel, geometric grille, or even prefab post caps and finials can add pizzazz to an otherwise mundane lineup of 2×2 balusters.

DISCOVERING YOUR STYLE

If you can't decide how you want your deck to look, start searching for ideas close to home. Your neighborhood can often provide you with the clues you need. Walk around one or two neighboring blocks and make notes of what you like. You'll be surprised at what you haven't noticed before. Clip photos from landscaping magazines and look through books about outdoor design. Then spread your notes and photo clips out on the dining room table and incorporate whatever appeals to you into your own design.

HARMONIZE YOUR LANDSCAPE

Individual elements in a good design create a unified whole. Base design continuity on the lines and colors of your house. A platform deck running parallel with a ranch house creates a harmony of horizontal lines, for example. A deck with lots of levels and angles would fit nicely with a West Coast modular but maybe not behind a three-story Victorian house, where a design reminiscent of a porch and railing might be more harmonious.

Look for color cues too. Paint, although not as often found on decks as stain or natural finish, can be the great equalizer, unifying house, deck, and outbuildings.

Select furnishings that support the dominant design. Use small elements to bring contrasts of color, shape, or texture. Gardens, edgings, walls, stone, tiles, bricks, logs, gates, furniture, lights, and decorative pieces—all add pleasing and lively accents.

Deck configurations

Decks can be almost any shape, but the shape of your deck should not be an arbitrary choice. Design the shape to conform to the terrain of your landscape, the architecture of your home, and how you plan to use the deck.

The least complicated installation will feature a ground-level deck—ideal for a flat yard and single-story home. Because this design hugs the ground, codes may not require a railing. Combine overlapping sections to make a deck cascade down a gentle slope.

Beyond the simple ground-level platform, decks fall into the three categories illustrated on this page.

Wraparound deck

A wraparound deck faces two or more sides of the house. It's ideal when you want quiet areas and space for large parties all on one deck. Wraparound decks also offer a solution for backyards that get different amounts of sunlight throughout the day. They offer great versatility for families who want outdoor space for a variety of needs. You can build a wraparound deck as a single ground-level platform, as a multilevel structure, or as a raised deck with second-story access.

Multilevel deck

Multilevel decks can have sections with different sizes and shapes. They provide a practical solution for sloping terrain, but you don't have to build a multilevel deck on a slope. A section can be on flat ground with steps to another deck on an upper level of your home. Consider this design when you need different deck areas for different outdoor activities.

Elevated deck

An elevated deck can be accessed from upper-level rooms or create a level recreational or entertainment space on sloping terrain. The least complicated version of this structure is a single platform supported by posts of suitable height. You can build one to take advantage of a view you might not be able to see from a ground-level deck or to get above a view you would rather look over.

Wrapping decks around a house

Turning a corner or two is one of the simplest ways to add area to a deck and still keep spaces well defined and separate. You can have one area for large gatherings and another that is a private nook. Dual use is the answer when you want access from more than one doorway.

Decks that wrap around a house increase costs only moderately and add few complications to construction. A wraparound is essentially two decks, with two ledgers and a common beam that unites both sections.

A modest wraparound could include a full-size deck on one side of the house with a small ell on an adjacent side, perhaps to be used for storage. More ambitious decks might surround two or three sides of the house on two or more levels. A narrow deck can serve as a walkway. On sloping lots, wraparound decks make moving around the perimeter of the house much easier.

Second-story porch
A wraparound deck provides plenty of room for family gatherings and private retreats. The deck style complements the home.

Sweeping veranda
This rambling deck features a generous walkway and several areas for lounging and dining, making it ideal for a variety of uses.

Wrapping decks around a house *(continued)*

Work with obstacles

This expansive deck demonstrates the value of working with obstacles, not against them. Extra framing allows the deck to follow the exterior walls of the home and surround the shade tree that's an important focal point. Wrapping the deck around the house as well as other elements in the yard creates a dramatic design. All of the details—French doors, tall windows, and repeated lattice patterns—help blend indoor and outdoor spaces.

WHEN A DECK IS NOT A DECK

Tradition says that porches are for the front of houses and decks are for the back. But the differences between a porch and a deck are largely theoretical. On older houses porches are often partially enclosed and are usually fully integrated into the facade, sometimes even continuing the roofline of the house. That kind of design integration is also important for a deck so it doesn't seem like an afterthought.

Fanciful outpost

If attaching a deck to the house would destroy the lines that make the house attractive, a detached deck might work. You don't need much space—a 10-foot octagon will provide enough space for family members to chat. A front yard structure is more open to public view than a backyard deck, so plan to build privacy screens or make use of existing ones, such as a high fence covered with vines.

Decks for any situation

Many lots have proportions or terrain that are not ideal for deck construction. Narrow properties, shallow yards, steep slopes, or dreary views may make building a deck seem difficult. However, design opportunities may be concealed inside a problem.

Often a deck can cover unusable outdoor space, such as a steep slope or small side yard, adding a comfortable and functional feature to your house.

Solutions to serious site problems may require a professional designer or licensed contractor. Even if you must call in the professionals, it's a good idea to develop preliminary plans of what you want to do with your deck space. That way the designer can base a proposal on the needs of your family as well as the limitations of the site.

Use all of a narrow lot

Decks for narrow lots with close neighbors often are only as wide as the house. This deck completely fills a narrow city lot, putting a limited front yard to good use.

High screens wrapping the structure keep the deck area private and buffer unwanted street noise.

Build long and narrow on a shallow lot

A lot that doesn't lend itself to an expansive deck shouldn't stop you from building. This long, narrow deck wraps around the corner of the house and includes a new stone walk that connects it to the front of the house. The design centers on a sliding door for access to the family room and includes lattice panels to screen the deck from the street. A patio extends the usable space while adding an extra level.

Decks for any situation *(continued)*

Block an unsightly view

The edges of a neighboring yard often become a storage area for things the neighbors don't want to see. This unsightly stuff may be invisible from the neighbor's outdoor living space but right up against yours. If the storage space is not likely to move, you can hide the view with screening.

This deck includes an attached privacy fence and its orientation and seating direct the views and traffic flow away from the lot next door.

Take advantage of a steep slope

Steep slopes can be an advantage and a disadvantage. Because the ground drops quickly away from the house, a deck on a steep slope can offer spectacular, sweeping views. This kind of deck can be more difficult to build. Whether the ground slopes down or up from the deck site, a multilevel deck that follows the contour of the landscape is often the best solution.

CAUTION

CONSULT LOCAL CODES
Elevated decks on steep slopes require well-engineered foundations and framing. You may need to assess soil integrity, drainage, or earthquake vulnerability. Before building on a steep slope, check with local building officials; you might need to consult a landscape architect or engineer.

New life for old decks

If you already have a deck but it's unappealing, you might be able to improve it instead of tearing it down and starting over.

If the deck is large and bland, divide it into smaller, more attractive spaces with planters, benches, or furniture.

If your deck is too small for the large gatherings you would like to have, build a detached freestanding deck and link the two with a boardwalk. Often a small platform, built in a style similar to the old deck, will fix the problem. Finish the new structure so it blends in with the old. Installing a brick patio beside or around an old deck may also help.

Open up the views to make a deck seem larger. Remove tall hedges or trim and thin them if you won't lose privacy. Replace a dense hedge with trellises and vines for an airier look or move fences and screens farther from the deck.

Conversely if you feel you're on display while meditating on the deck, shield the area with a fence or shrubs. If the visual intrusion comes from a second story, add an overhead structure.

Clean up the view. Gather unsightly utility items—garbage cans, compost bins, and loose yard tools—into a fenced service area or garden shed. Build an attractive screen around the air-conditioner and utility equipment.

A new railing and better stairs will often revive an old deck. Post lights at the corners or rope lights under the railing lend a magical air at night. Clean and paint or refinish the deck and railings for a new look.

Build on what you have. Instead of trying to add a fire pit into a deck that's already cramped, extend the deck or build a satellite deck to accommodate this new amenity.

Clear a path
If your deck is underused, it may only need a little rearranging. Furnishings in the middle of a natural pathway take an area out of service. Move them to the sides of the deck, leaving the central area open.

Preparing for the project

The transition from theory to practice can be the most difficult phase of a deck building project. This is where questions may start to concern you.
- Will the deck be big enough?
- Does it fit my budget?
- Do I have the skills needed to build it?

Consider the questions carefully and try to answer them thoroughly before proceeding. Don't rush into the project;

think through all of the consequences and procedures. If you've only recently moved into the house, it might be too soon to build a deck. By waiting a year you will be able to observe the house through all the seasonal changes and a variety of weather conditions.

Budgeting is a tricky—and highly personal—part of the project. With thorough planning, however, you can avoid surprises. As long as you are supplying the labor, you can determine

your expenses by preparing a detailed list of materials (drawn from your equally detailed plans) to take to several suppliers for estimates. With an idea of costs, you can decide whether you want to borrow the money and build today or save money to build later.

Deck building is straightforward work, but parts of it are physically demanding and all of it requires close attention to detail. If you are concerned about your own ability to build the deck you want, determine which parts of the job most trouble you. Perhaps you worry about getting the ledger installed correctly and the posts set straight and true. If so, act as a general contractor and subcontract those parts of the job. You may be able to hire an experienced carpenter to work with you on all or part of the job. This apprenticeship may be all you need to boost your confidence for your next project.

TAKE A SHORTCUT

- Various time- and moneysaving services are available at your local home center or lumberyard. Many retailers sell standard deck plans, either individually or in books. If you find a plan that you like and your building site presents no problems, the cost of published plans can be money well spent.

- Some larger home centers and lumberyards offer complete packages for standard deck sizes at attractive prices. If you want a plain deck without custom features and your deck site is relatively flat and presents few problems, you may save time and money with a deck kit.

Preparing for the project *(continued)*

Before you start building call the utility companies and have them mark underground lines in your yard. This will show you where it's safe to dig holes for posts.

Take your time and complete all the planning before ordering lumber. When the lumber truck backs into your yard, you should have a building permit in hand, a clear idea of what your deck will look like, and a plan for who's going to do the work.

MAKE A CONSTRUCTION SCHEDULE

Make a construction schedule to keep track of all the tasks you have to complete. Each list will be different, but most will include these steps:
- Conduct site analysis.
- Draw plans and elevations.
- Apply for building permit.
- Finalize materials list and costs.
- Modify plan as necessary and schedule inspections.
- Order materials.
- Strip sod and prepare site.
- Attach ledger.
- Set batterboards; lay out site.
- Dig footings; set posts.
- Hang beams and joists.
- Fasten decking.
- Build railings and stairs.
- Apply deck finish.

PLAY IT SAFE

Elements that make decks interesting—stairways, railings, hot tubs, high elevations—create safety hazards, especially for children. Compliance with local codes and zoning restrictions won't guarantee a safe deck. These requirements represent minimum standards; your particular situation may demand more. Lessen the risk with a few simple precautions:

- When building a deck railing, space the balusters no more than 4 inches apart, even if your local code allows wider spacing.
- Treat deck stairs as you do indoor stairs; if young children are present, put a gate at the top. Put another one at the bottom if the stairs lead to a part of the house or another area you don't want children to enter.
- If you install built-in benches, make the railings behind them at least 24 inches above the seat to prevent a child from climbing or falling over the side.
- Before you design railings with horizontal infill, such as piping, check with your building department officials. Codes may prohibit them because children can use them as a ladder to climb over the railing.
- Fence off a hot tub or spa and install a childproof gate. If that's not practical, use a secure cover.

PREVENT ROT AND WATER DAMAGE

Position butt joints over doubled joists.

Flash the ledger.

Use pressure-treated or rot-resistant wood throughout.

Seal the deck often.

Coat ends with preservative.

Keep post ends off concrete.

Rot can ruin a deck. Rot-producing fungi thrive in wood that always stays moist. Here are some ways to protect your deck from moisture:
- Set posts in metal brackets so they won't make contact with the earth or concrete.
- A built-up beam (a beam using two separate boards) lasts longer if you use moisture-draining spacers (see page 70).

- Incorporate butt joints into the decking so that water can drain. Position the joints over doubled joists with spacers between them to provide a path for water to drain.
- Pay attention to flashing around the ledger.
- Brush extra preservative on all cut ends of pressure-treated lumber, especially the ends of support and railing posts.

Drawing plans

All you need to make accurate deck plans are a pencil, ruler, and graph paper. A dimensioned plan that's drawn to scale will help you calculate costs, order materials, and keep your construction on schedule. You'll probably also need a plan to submit to the building department for approval.

Draw your deck to scale on graph paper (typically ¼ inch to the foot). You'll need at least a site plan, a plan (overhead) view, and one or two elevations. You can also draw detailed plans for complex parts of the deck. Drawing plans can be tedious, but it helps make the project go smoothly.

DRAFTING TOOLBOX

You can draw a deck plan quickly with these tools:

- A pad of graph paper (use a ¼-inch grid) and tracing paper
- Drafting tape (to hold the paper down)
- Two or three No. 3 pencils (the harder lead makes more precise lines than No. 2s)
- A good eraser
- A 12-inch ruler, circle templates, and an architect's scale

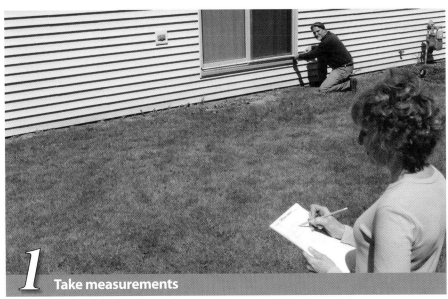

1 Take measurements

Deck plans begin with measurements of your property. Take a 100-foot tape (and a pad and pencil) into your yard and measure the house and the distance from the house to the property lines. Mark locations of windows and doors, outside electrical outlets, dryer vents, utility connections, and water valves.

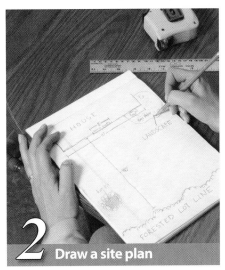

2 Draw a site plan

A site plan shows your property boundaries, the house, and other major features. It also shows the distances between elements in your landscape that might affect the construction of your deck. A simple deck plan only needs to be a sketch that includes these measurements. More complicated deck plans will require a scale drawing.

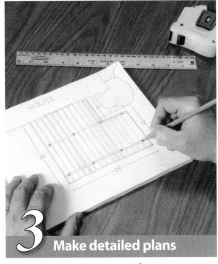

3 Make detailed plans

Detailed plans show every framing member so you can count the pieces of lumber you need. You can also show obstacles such as dryer vents; plans will help you work around them. Detailed plans can save you money. Because lumber is sold in even lengths, you can keep costs down by making deck dimensions correspond to these lengths. If your detailed plan calls for a 12½-foot ledger and you can reduce it to 12 feet, you'll avoid cutting a 14-foot board and wasting 18 inches of lumber.

Drawing plans *(continued)*

- 2×6 decking
- Ledger
- 12'
- 20'
- Beam
- 4×4 post
- 12" cantilever
- Double joist at decking butt joint
- Double joist at decking butt joint
- 2×8 joists, 16" on center

Complete a plan (overhead) view

A plan view shows the deck as seen from above. It lays out the exact location of posts, beams, and joists. It may also include a partial view of the decking, railing, and any other structures attached to the deck. The drawing above combines a view of the framing with the decking installed above the beams and posts. For more complex decks these two views can be drawn separately. Draw the support and framing plan first, then use tracing paper to produce the finished view.

Include all dimensions—overall length and width, joist and beam spacing, and material sizes.

- Baluster spacing
- Railing height
- Joist span
- Deck width
- Footing depth
- Post and beam height

Draw elevation (side or front) view

A front or side elevation illustrates the vertical arrangement of deck elements—footings, posts, railings, and any built-in planters, benches, or overhead structures. Each elevation should show the depth of the footings, spans, and post and railing dimensions. Railing dimensions should indicate the height of the railing as well as baluster spacing.

Tools, Materials, and Techniques

New materials, standard tools

Conventional tools such as this circular saw work well for cutting synthetic and composite decking as well as wood. See the proper techniques for using a circular saw on pages 33–34. Pages 41–43 contain information about lumber and synthetic materials.

Going cordless

You'll need a power drill to drill holes and drive screws, but corded or cordless? A cordless drill/driver (with enough power and a backup battery) is a better choice for most chores. A variable-speed reversible cordless drill/driver makes short work of screwing down decking.

CAUTION

WORKSITE SAFETY

Worksite safety is based on following guidelines and exercising common sense. Hand tools can hurt you, and power tools used improperly can be dangerous. But there's no reason to fear them if you follow these guidelines:

- Use tools only for the tasks they were designed for. Take time to read the tool's instruction manual to find out what the tool can and cannot do.
- Check on the condition of a tool before using it. A dull cutting blade or a loose hammerhead, for example, can be dangerous. Inspect the cord of a power tool to make sure it's not damaged.
- Don't work with tools if you're tired or in a hurry.
- Don't work with tools if you have been drinking alcoholic beverages that day.

- Wear safety goggles, a dust mask, ear protectors, gloves, and work shoes or boots when appropriate for the task.
- The safety mechanisms on power tools are there for your protection. Do not tamper with them or remove them from the tool.
- Do not wear loose-fitting clothes or dangling jewelry while you are using tools.
- Keep other people, especially children, at a safe distance.

Essential tools

These tools will come in handy at various stages of the project; add the ones you don't have to your tool kit. You can use most of them for other projects after the deck is finished, so buy high-quality tools. Avoid inexpensive tools, which often break, wear out quickly, don't stay sharp, and may be less comfortable to use.

Layout tools

Layout can be the most exacting aspect of deck building, but layout tools aren't expensive. Here's what you'll need:

Line level
This small level hangs on a mason's line so you can span distances too long to check with a carpenter's level.

Mason's line
For this mainstay of layout work, use nylon line; it's stronger and doesn't stretch as much as cotton twine.

Plumb bob
This hanging weight accurately indicates vertical. It's handy when you are marking posthole locations.

Steel tape
This is a do-it-yourselfer's constant companion. A 1-inch blade will extend farther without sagging. You'll need at least a 16-footer—a 25-footer will save you time.

Carpentry tools

These tools are the backbone of do-it-yourself carpentry. If you're assembling your tool chest for the first time, buy high-quality tools; you'll use them for other projects.

Adjustable clamp
Handy for holding pieces of lumber together for cutting, drilling, and more. Buy several; you rarely have too many clamps.

Adjustable wrench
Turns hex- or square-head bolts, nuts, and lag screws and holds a bolt head while you tighten the nut with another wrench.

C-clamp
These come in a variety of sizes for many jobs. Always buy at least two of any clamp.

Carpenter's level
Get a 48-inch model for checking plumb and level. Shorter versions may give false readings over long spans. Buy one with a rigid steel or aluminum frame.

Carpenter's pencil
To make visible lines use a chisel-pointed carpenter's pencil. Buy a sharpener for it too. For precise marking, however, use a standard pencil or mechanical pencil.

Cat's paw
This is the best tool for pulling nails.

Caulking gun
Dispenses caulk and adhesives from tubes. Get one with an easy tension release to prevent wasting material.

Chalkline and chalk
Snap a chalkline to lay out a straight line between two points.

Chisel
Essential for cleaning out notches. Buy high-quality chisels and take good care of them. Sharp chisels make clean, accurate cuts for good-fitting joints. Drive wood-handled chisels with a mallet, not a metal hammer.

Circular saw
Buy a heavy-duty saw with a 7¼-inch carbide-tipped combination blade. The saw will come in handy on a deck or any other project that requires cutting of framing members, boards, or sheet goods.

Combination square
Use this indispensable tool to check 90- and 45-degree angles quickly and to measure and lay out cutlines. You can adjust it to gauge a fixed distance from an edge too.

Essential tools *(continued)*

Cordless drill

This essential tool drills holes and drives screws. Buy at least a 14.4-volt model with a spare battery.

Framing hammer

Buy a high-quality 20-ounce hammer. The extra weight may seem tiring at first, but you'll appreciate it when driving 16d nails.

Framing square

You'll use this large square to square corners and to mark stair stringers.

Groove-joint pliers

Handy for gripping, holding, and pulling.

Handsaw

You'll need this for quick cuts and to finish corner cuts where a circular saw won't go.

Jigsaw

If you're cutting any fancy patterns, you'll need one of these. Buy a heavy-duty model.

Layout square

This triangular square helps you quickly lay out angled cuts or mark cutlines. It's tough and compact.

Locking pliers

This versatile tool holds, grips, and clamps.

Nail set

Use to set finishing nails in railings or trim.

Plane

A plane shaves wood off the edge of a board or chamfers sharp edges on a post or railing.

Post level

Strap this to a post to plumb it in two directions at once. Nothing does it better.

Power drill

A corded ⅜- or ½-inch electric drill has power to spare for drilling big holes. Buy a variable-speed reversing model.

Pry bar

This is handy when you need to force a warped board into place or to remove nails.

Sawhorses

Use these to support lumber for cutting.

Socket wrench

A ratchet handle with socket is the best tool for tightening nuts and lag screws.

Squeeze clamps

Inexpensive and quick to use, these are less likely to dent lumber.

T-bevel

This gauge adjusts to duplicate an angle.

Torpedo level

This short level fits in tighter spaces when a carpenter's level is too long.

Utility knife

With a retractable blade this knife will sharpen your pencils and trim materials.

Water level

This device shows level over long distances. Some attach to a garden hose.

Specialized tools

One of the decisions you have to make on a project is which, if any, new tools to buy. That's especially true of some of the specialized tools shown on this page.

Many do-it-yourselfers like to look at any project as an opportunity to add new tools to their collection. But remember that needing a tool doesn't always mean you have to buy it.

If you might not use a tool very often after your deck is done, you might be better off renting it. Estimate how often you'll need the tool later, then consider the cost of buying versus renting.

Framing tools

Hammer drill
Its dual drilling and hammering action makes drilling holes in masonry easy. This is handy if you need to install a ledger on masonry or set post bases.

Power nailer
A pneumatic framing nailer makes quick work of framing and attaching deck boards. You will need an air compressor with adequate capacity to power the nailer.

Reciprocating saw
This is the ideal tool for cutting posts to height after they have been set. It comes in handy for demolition and a variety of other tasks too.

RENTING TOOLS

When you need an expensive tool for only a short period or if you can't afford to buy it new, visit a tool rental store. A well-equipped rental store will have any tool you find in this book, including circular saws and drills.

When considering tool purchases it pays to compare the cost of buying a new tool versus renting one.

Tools are rented by the hour, day, or week. To avoid excessive charges don't pick up the tool until you need it. Clean the tool before returning it to prevent extra charges.

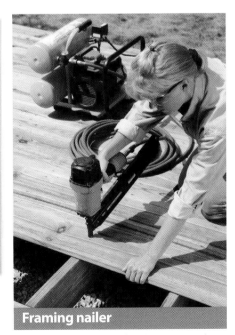

Framing nailer

This is a standard tool for the pros. Push the safety-lock shoe against the work and pull the trigger. The lock prevents the gun from accidentally discharging the nail.

Reciprocating saw

The saw blade moves back and forth, which can make the saw jump. Steady the saw with the shoe against the stock until you've cut completely through.

Specialized tools *(continued)*

Round-nose shovel · Clamshell digger · Hoe · Spade · Garden rake · Tamping bar · Wheelbarrow

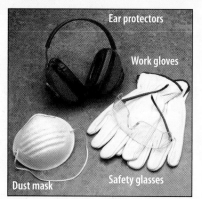
Tools for excavating and concrete

Clamshell digger: Dig straight-sided holes with the digger's hinged blades.
Garden rake: Level soil and smooth gravel with a standard rake.
Hoe: Get a mason's hoe with holes in the blade for mixing concrete.

Shovels: Excavate with a round-nose shovel, remove sod with a spade.
Tamping bar: Tamp soil when filling holes to minimize later settling.
Wheelbarrow: Haul materials or mix concrete in a wheelbarrow.

Digging postholes with power

A one-person power auger

A two-person power auger

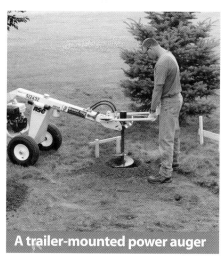

A trailer-mounted power auger

You'll need a trailer to haul some models home. Start the engine. Set the bit over the hole and lower it slowly, letting its weight do the work. Raise the bit periodically to clean it. Keep the bit turning when raising it from the hole. Add extensions for deeper holes.

Two-person motorized augers are more difficult to operate. Get detailed instructions when renting one. The torque can knock you off balance. Start the engine. You and your helper should plant your feet firmly before engaging the bit. Be braced for roots and rocks.

This hydraulically powered unit produces maximum boring power with minimum wear and tear on the operator. To ease the auger into the soil, you simply operate a control handle. The hydraulics of the unit do the lifting and lowering.

Measuring and marking

Accurate measuring and marking are essential to successful carpentry. A mistake in measuring usually results in wasted time and material. Although it may seem elementary, developing accurate measuring skills takes practice.

Don't rush your measurements; double-check them. Apply the age-old carpenter's maxim, "Measure twice, cut once."

No matter what measuring device you use, become familiar with it and learn how to read it accurately. Learn to immediately recognize the ¼-inch and ⅛-inch increments. Many a board has been ruined because the carpenter misread the mark. Once you've made a measurement, jot it down on paper, a wood scrap, or the board itself.

Carpentry rarely calls for precision greater than ¹⁄₁₆ inch. That's because it's difficult to cut more precisely than that with a circular saw. A tape measure with ¹⁄₃₂-inch marks for the first few inches is not essential, and sometimes those tiny increments can be distracting.

Often it's the marking, not the measuring, that introduces error. Wide marks are less precise. Make a clear mark with a sharp No. 2 pencil, the thin edge of a sharpened carpenter's pencil, a knife, or a scratch awl.

USE A SINGLE TAPE

Different measuring tapes may disagree, varying by up to ⅛ inch. Use one tape for all measuring and marking. If you are taking measurements and giving them to a partner who is using another tape to mark and cut lumber, compare the tapes to be sure they read the same.

Take an outside measurement

To take an outside measurement, hook the tape over the outside edge of the board. Make sure you have engaged the board with the tang of the hook and not the rivets that hold it in place. Pull the case of the tape toward the point you want to measure. Set the blade of the tape against the outside point and read the tape where it intersects the edge. Write the measurement on paper or a piece of scrap lumber. Some tape measures have a place for writing measurements on the case.

Take an inside measurement

To measure the space between framing members, first hook the tape over the outside edge of one of the boards (or run it out by hand) as if you were taking an outside measurement. Pull the case just past the point you wish to measure and lock the blade. Then lift the hook off the board and push it against the inside face of the board near the edge. Read the tape where it intersects the inside face of the other board. Jot down the measurement.

Measuring and marking *(continued)*

Marking rip cuts

Measure the width of the cut on both ends of the board, then snap a chalkline between the marks or use a straightedge to connect them with a pencil line.

Layout square

Marking miter cuts

Set a square flush against the edge of the board at the point you wish to cut. (When marking the end of a board, pull the edge of the square down slightly from the corner.) Hold it steady and mark the line.

Marking onsite

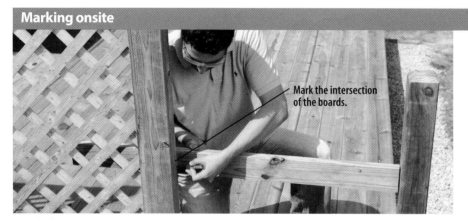

Mark the intersection of the boards.

Onsite measurements are usually more accurate than those taken with tapes. Whenever possible hold the board to be cut in position, then mark the cutline.

Marking crosscuts

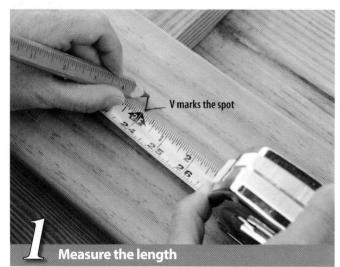

V marks the spot

1 Measure the length

Extend the tape from the squared end of the board to the point where you will make the cut. Mark the measurement with a V, placing the point of the V at the measurement.

Layout square

Point of V mark

2 Extend the mark

Hold the tip of your pencil on the point of the V mark and slide a layout square along the edge of the board until it touches the pencil tip. Run your pencil along the square.

Squaring, plumbing, and leveling

All carpentry projects have elements that must be square, plumb, or level. These characteristics are important to the appearance of a structure, and they increase its structural integrity. A deck that is not square, plumb, and level may collapse.

Depending on what part of the project is involved, you can make sure your construction meets these criteria with a variety of tools. Most aren't complicated, but you should treat them carefully.

If the edge on a combination square is damaged or worn, you won't get a square reading. The same is true for a bent or worn framing square. If the vials in a level are out of alignment, your level won't level. Check squares against a known 90-degree corner (the factory corner of a 4×8 sheet of plywood, for example). Test a level by leveling a board with it, then turning the level around. It should show level both ways. If you can't repair or adjust an inaccurate tool, buy a new one before you start the project.

THE MULTIPURPOSE LAYOUT SQUARE

Almost every carpenter's belt has a hammer, utility knife, pencil, and the ever-handy layout square. With a triangular layout square, you can quickly mark 45- and 90-degree angles simply by holding the square with its body firmly against a true edge. Other angles are stamped on the body of the square and can be laid out with a fair degree of accuracy. In addition the layout square is a handy guide for cutting with a circular saw (see page 34).

QUICK CHECK

To check a rectangular structure for square, measure diagonally between the corners. If the two diagonal measurements are the same, the structure is square.

Framing square

Use a framing square to square large corners—the header and rim joist, for example. Place the square inside or outside the corner and look along the lengths of both the tongue (short side) and the blade (long side). They should fit flush against the boards along their entire lengths. If you see light, adjust the boards until the square fits snugly. Don't be satisfied if only the corner of the square is tight. The framing is not true unless the square fits snugly along the entire lengths of the tongue and blade.

3-4-5 triangle

This method is handy when laying out sites or when a corner is too large for a framing square. Measure 3 feet out from the corner on one side and mark the measurement precisely with tape. Measure out 4 feet on the other side and mark it. Have a helper hold the end of a tape measure on one mark, then measure to the other. If the distance between them is 5 feet, the corner is square. If it's not, adjust the corner angle and measure again. Multiples of 3, 4, and 5 feet—such as 6, 8, and 10 or 15, 20, and 25—are even more accurate.

Squaring, plumbing, and leveling *(continued)*

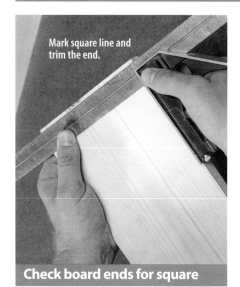

Check board ends for square

Careful measuring will be wasted on a piece of lumber that is not square; one edge will be longer than the other. Check the board end by holding a combination or layout square firmly against a factory edge. If the end isn't square, mark a square line and trim the board.

Extending a square line

Some installations require extending a level or square line to other faces of a board. A combination square or layout square will help you do this quickly. Slide the square on an unmarked face until it reaches the level line you've marked. Transfer this line to the unmarked face and repeat for other faces.

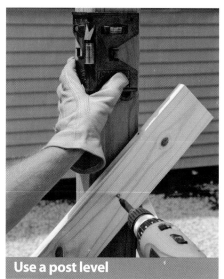

Use a post level

Deck posts must be plumb in two planes at the same time. You can plumb them one side at a time with a carpenter's level, but a post level with two vials plumbs both sides at once. Strap or hold the level on the post and brace the post when the bubbles in both vials are centered.

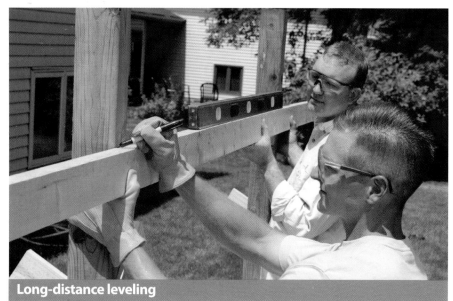

Long-distance leveling

When you need to mark or extend a level line over more than 6 feet, use a water level or a level on a straight board. A laser level will also work well if it projects a line bright enough to be seen in the sun.

A water level uses the principle that water will find the same level over any distance. Two pieces of clear plastic tubing fastened to the ends of a water-filled hose show the water level at both ends. Hold the ends of the level against both surfaces and mark the boards at the waterline. The water level can be used around corners.

You can also set (or better yet, tape) a carpenter's level to a straight board to extend a level line. Hold the board against the line at one end, adjust the board to center the bubble in the vial, and mark the other end. Using this method is easier if you have someone to help.

Plumbing with a level

A carpenter's level has vials at each end set perpendicular to its frame. Use these vials for plumbing a board when no other method will work—when plumbing the face of a ledger, for example. Hold the level vertically against the board and adjust the board until the bubble in the end vial (the top one) is centered.

Cutting with a circular saw

Circular saws are so versatile and convenient that it's hard to imagine building a deck without one. Today's saws are lightweight and relatively inexpensive, and double insulation reduces the danger of electric shock.

You will probably cut most of your deck lumber with a circular saw. Whether crosscutting 1× stock, ripping plywood, or cutting bricks with a masonry blade, you'll do the job better if you follow a few basic rules when using this tool.

Allow the saw to reach full operating speed away from the wood, then slowly push the blade into the wood. Some carpenters look at the blade as they cut; others rely on the gunsight notch. Choose the method that's most comfortable for you. Don't let the blade wander—find the straight path and push the saw through the wood smoothly. You'll need some practice before you can do this consistently. Don't wear loose sleeves and don't get your face near the saw, trying to see a line, for example.

Support the material

Well-supported work results in clean, safe cuts. Support the board so the saw won't bind or kick back and to keep the end of the board from splintering as the waste falls away. If the waste piece is short, support just the good end of the board.

If the waste end is longer than 2 feet, support the board in four places so neither end of the board will bind the blade and you can make a straight, neat cut. Support the lumber in four places for best results on all cuts.

CHOOSING A CIRCULAR SAW AND BLADES

Choose a saw with adequate power (one that draws about 15 amps) that you can hold comfortably. You should be able to see the blade and gunsight notch in the baseplate easily. Depth and bevel adjustments should move easily and stay put.

If you buy only one blade for a circular saw, choose a carbide-tipped combination blade with 24 teeth. It works well for rough work and makes crosscuts and ripcuts clean enough for most finish work. For finer work, such as cutting cap-rail miters, buy a blade with 40 or more teeth.

CAUTION

AVOIDING KICKBACK

It can happen to even the most experienced carpenter: The blade binds, causing the saw to jump backward. That's called kickback, and it can mar the lumber you are working on or cause injury as you lose control of the saw. Unsupported stock often is the problem, but these are some other possibilities:

- A dull blade will bind and kick the saw back. Change your blade or get it sharpened if you have to push hard to make it cut.
- Bent or twisted lumber will grab a blade. Sheets of plywood are particularly prone to bending while being cut. Make sure your stock is evenly supported.

- Kickback also can occur when you back up the saw while cutting or when you try to cut a turn. If your saw gets off line, stop it, back up, and start again.
- Occasionally the grain of the wood will grab the blade and cause kickback. The only thing you can do about this is be prepared for it.

Cutting with a circular saw *(continued)*

SET THE BLADE DEPTH

Before you make a cut, set the blade to extend no more than ¼ inch past the thickness of the wood. (Be sure to unplug the saw before you do this.) Release the saw plate latch to position the plate to the proper depth.

This may seem like a lot of bother, especially if you are frequently switching between cutting 1× and 2× lumber. But it's worth the trouble because a saw blade that extends only slightly below the material will produce a much cleaner cut than a blade that extends way below the material.

The deeper the blade is set, the more prone it will be to binding and kickback, endangering the work and your safety.

Square the blade

Even on a new, factory-set saw, the blade may not be square to the saw plate. That will produce beveled cuts. To square the blade unplug the saw, hold a layout or try square against the blade (between the teeth) and the plate, and adjust the plate until you can't see light between the blade and the square.

Align the blade with the cutline

Once you have drawn an accurate cutoff line and have properly supported the board, position the saw blade on the scrap side of the line. The teeth on most circular saw blades are offset in an alternating pattern, half to the left and half to the right. When clamping a guide align a tooth that points toward the cutoff line.

Guide the cut with a square

With practice you will learn to cut accurately without a guide. For now, and for precise cuts, guide the cut with a square. For 90-degree cuts a layout square works well because its heel plate keeps it stable. Line up the blade with the cut, then slide the square up against the saw plate. Hold the board and the square with your free hand to keep them steady.

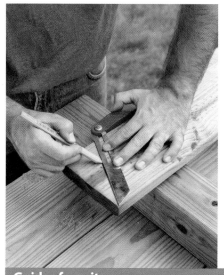

Guides for miters

With care you can improvise a saw guide that will be as accurate as a miter box. Set a T-bevel to the correct angle and transfer the angle to the board.

Clamp a straight piece of 1× stock parallel to the cutline and at a distance that will put the saw blade just on the waste side of the cutline. It may take some experimenting before you get everything to line up properly. Measure the distance

from the blade to the edge of the saw plate (many come from the factory already marked). Use this to mark your parallel line for the guide.

For long rip cuts, clamp the factory edge of a 1× board or a drywall square to the material, setting it back from the cutline to allow for the distance from the edge of the saw plate to the blade.

Drilling

The electric drill (either corded or cordless) is today's preferred tool for drilling holes. In fact the cordless drill/driver can help with so many tasks that it ranks as everyone's basic power tool. With a variable-speed reversible cordless drill/driver, you can drill a hole of about any size, drive screws into wood or metal, buff and grind, and even mix paint.

A drill is not as dangerous as a circular saw, but you still need to keep safety in mind as you use it. Always wear safety goggles (the kind with side protectors) when you are drilling. Insert the bit or accessory fully into the chuck and tighten the chuck jaws firmly. Clamp the workpiece if you can—the bit can bind and cause a piece to spin, causing injury. Don't force the drill; allow its speed to do the work.

CHOOSING A DRILL

- Avoid buying a low-quality power drill or any light-duty model with a ¼-inch chuck.
- A cordless drill can make your work easier but only if it is powerful enough to do most things that a corded drill can do. Any cordless drill under 14.4 volts probably won't have the power you need. An 18-volt model is better. Get two batteries for any cordless drill.
- A drill with a ⅜-inch chuck is ideal for most household tasks (including building a deck). Larger drills will have more power, but they're harder to handle and you'll rarely need that power.

- Buy a variable-speed, reversible drill. Tasks often require variable drilling speeds and reversing capability. Most high-quality models have both.
- A keyless chuck is a great timesaver that allows you to tighten the bit in the chuck by twisting its nose. Do a little research on this feature; some keyless chucks hold bits better than others.
- Get a model with a two-speed transmission—one for drilling and the other for driving screws.
- A hammer drill combines the rotary action of a drill with the percussive action of a hammer. It's the best kind for drilling concrete and masonry.

Make a starting mark

Twist drills tend to skate off the center mark when they begin turning, so give them a starting dimple with an awl or a center punch. Set the tip of the bit into the punch mark, start the drill slowly, and increase the speed as it bites into the wood.

Keep chips from clogging holes

When you drill deep holes into thick material, wood chips build up in the hole, which can clog the bit and cause it to bind. Don't force the bit. Instead withdraw the bit from the hole frequently while the drill is running. This will pull trapped wood chips to the surface. If you're working

with sappy or moist wood, shavings may clog the flute of the bit. If this happens withdraw the drill and stop it. Then clean out the flute with the tip of a nail. If the bit jams, reverse the drill rotation and pull the bit straight out.

Drilling *(continued)*

Improvise a guide

Mark the bit for depth

Most holes are drilled perpendicular to the surface of the wood. You can easily help keep the bit square by clamping a piece of scrap next to the hole. Start the bit in the hole, then move the scrap to it and clamp it.

When you need to drill a hole at an angle, make a guide by cutting a piece

of scrap to the same angle. Clamp the guide so it aligns the tip of the bit exactly on your center mark. Begin by drilling perpendicular to the surface. Once you have gone deep enough to keep the bit from skating away, angle the drill.

When you want to drill a couple of holes to a specific depth, put tape around the bit at the depth of the hole. Back the bit out as soon as the tape touches the wood. For consistent depth over a large number of holes, use depth stops. These collars are matched to the size of the bit, and a locknut keeps them in place.

CAUTION

AVOID DAMAGING YOUR DRILL BITS AND DRILL

Drilling is a basic procedure, but it's easy to dull or break a drill bit. Be careful not to overheat the bit; an overheated bit will become dull quickly. If you see smoke, stop drilling immediately. Pause once in a while and tap the bit with your finger to see if it's hot.

Hold the drill firmly upright as you work. If you wobble the tool while drilling, the bit may break.

DRILLING MASONRY AND CONCRETE

Use a masonry bit when drilling into brick or concrete. Check the bit often to make sure it's not overheating. If you see smoke, stop immediately.

Here is a trick that works surprisingly well: Spray the bit and the hole with window cleaner as you work. This keeps the bit cool, and the foaming of the cleaner helps bring debris out of the hole.

When drilling into concrete you may run into an especially hard spot (usually a rock embedded in the concrete). Take the bit out, insert a masonry nail or thin cold chisel, and with a hammer, crack the rock. That will give your bit a place to grab. If you have a lot of masonry drilling to do, buy or rent a hammer drill.

DOUBLE DRILL BOLT HOLES

A spade bit tears the wood as it drills through the backside. For clean bores use this two-step technique. Choose a bit slightly larger than the bolt diameter. Drill through one side until the tip just breaks through. Then finish drilling the hole from the other side.

PREDRILL FASTENERS

Whenever you drive a nail or screw less than 2 inches from the edge of a board, drill a pilot hole to protect against splitting the board. Use a drill bit slightly smaller than the diameter of the fastener.

Using a tablesaw

A tablesaw is the centerpiece of many workshops and can make many aspects of deck construction go more quickly by producing more accurate cuts.

You can build a deck without a tablesaw, but if you need to rip long boards, cut notches or dadoes, or miter clean corners in your top rail, a tablesaw is the best tool.

A tablesaw rugged enough for deck work will more than return its cost in time and convenience. And the saw works well for many home improvement projects.

The accuracy of a tablesaw depends on the table, fence, and miter gauge. Check the table for flatness with a long straightedge. The rip fence on a tablesaw should slide smoothly, lock into position easily, and stay locked. The blade height and tilt adjustments should move easily and stay at the same settings until you move them. Look for a miter gauge that slides smoothly without play in the table slots.

Adjust the blade height

Adjust the blade height to extend about ¼ inch above the top face of the board you are cutting. This makes a cleaner cut and helps avoid binding and kickback. If you are cutting a sheet of warped plywood, you may need to raise the blade higher so it will cut completely through the sheet. Always unplug the tablesaw before making blade adjustments.

CAUTION

SAFETY MEASURES FOR A TABLESAW

Because a tablesaw has so much power and cuts so quickly, you need to focus on the task when you are using one. An instant's inattention can cause an accident to occur.

Always keep your fingers well away from the blade. Never wear gloves, long sleeves, or loose clothing while using a tablesaw. Never reach across the saw blade while it is running. Keep push sticks and antikickback featherboards handy and get into the habit of using them (see instructions on this page).

Turn the saw off when you need to free a piece of wood that has become stuck. Lower the blade below the table and unplug the saw when you're done for the day.

TABLESAW, RADIAL ARM SAW, OR POWER MITERSAW?

A tablesaw and a power mitersaw make an ideal combination. You can easily make long, straight cuts with a tablesaw. A tablesaw also is best for cutting dadoes. With a power mitersaw you can crosscut long, narrow pieces easily.

A radial arm saw does what a tablesaw and power mitersaw can, but not quite as well. It crosscuts with less precision than a mitersaw and can bind on miter cuts. Radial arm saws do not make ripcuts well. They frequently kick the board back. Use your tablesaw for ripcuts.

Antikickback featherboard

Push stick

Backer for support

Use push sticks and a featherboard

To make a featherboard cut one end of a 16-inch-long 1×6 to 60 degrees, then cut 8-inch-long kerfs ¼ inch apart on the angled end. Clamp so it holds stock against the fence ahead of the blade to ensure a straight cut and prevent kickback if the blade binds. Make push sticks out of 1× lumber or ½-inch plywood and use them whenever you need to hold the board within 6 inches of the blade.

Using a tablesaw *(continued)*

Make a ripcut

Check that the fence is perfectly parallel to the blade by measuring the space between the blade and the fence at the front and the rear of the blade. Set the blade height ¼ inch above the top of the board. Start the motor and allow it to reach full speed. Hold the board flush against the fence and keep it that way as you push it forward. Never allow your fingers to come within 6 inches of the blade; use a push stick when you come to the end of the cut (see page 37).

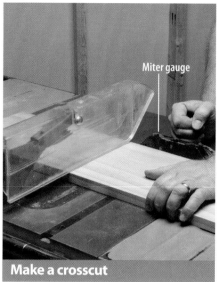

Miter gauge

Make a crosscut

Make sure the miter gauge is exactly perpendicular to the blade; slip it into its channel and square it to the blade (do this with the saw unplugged). Set the blade height to ¼ inch above the board and start the motor. Hold the board firmly against the miter gauge and push the board into the blade. Hold the board only at the miter gauge and never use the fence with the gauge. Holding a board on both sides of the cut may bind the blade and cause kickback.

Make a bevel ripcut

To set the bevel use the saw gauge or mark the bevel angle on the butt end of the board, then tilt the blade until it aligns with the mark. Hold the board against the blade at the correct location, slide the fence against the board, and lock the fence into position. Follow the same procedures as for a ripcut.

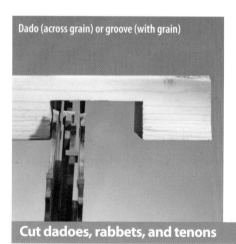

Dado (across grain) or groove (with grain)

Rabbet

Tenon made with an adjustable dado blade

Cut dadoes, rabbets, and tenons

You can make a variety of wide cuts with a dado blade. With a regular dado blade, sandwich a combination of chippers between the two outside cutter blades to your desired width. On an adjustable dado set the width by turning the blade hub. To set the cutting depth for either type, mark the depth on the board and hold it next to the blade as you adjust the blade elevation.

If you need to make a cut wider than the dado blade, make repeated passes, moving the board a little less than the width of the blade with each pass.

You will not be able to see the cut as you make it on a tablesaw, so test your settings on a scrap piece to make sure the dado is the correct width and depth before you make the real cut.

Cutting with a handsaw

Although power tools make accurate cutting relatively easy, sometimes a handsaw is more convenient—even necessary. For example, when you have only a few cuts to make in thin stock, a handsaw might be faster than getting out the circular saw and setting it up. And you can start stair stringer cuts with a circular saw, but you'll need a handsaw to complete them.

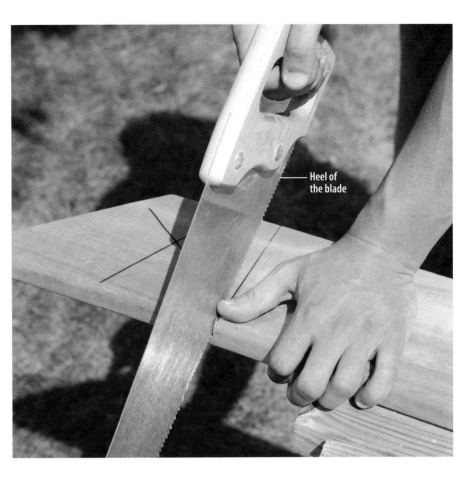

Heel of the blade

Making crosscuts

To make a crosscut with a handsaw, set the heel of the blade at a 45-degree angle to the workpiece with the teeth on the waste side of the cutline. Use your thumbnail to keep the blade from wandering. Pull the saw straight back several times to start the cut. Don't force the blade; use the weight of the saw to set the pace of the work. Saw with a rocking motion, using a steeper angle at the beginning of the downstroke and a flatter angle at its completion. Again, don't force it; let the saw set the pace.

Finish the cut cleanly

When you're near the end of the cut, support the waste end of the wood. Grasp it firmly with your free hand, exerting a slight upward pressure to keep it from binding. This also will keep the piece from snapping and splintering on the last stroke.

Make a cutout

To notch the corner of a board, bring the blade of the saw perpendicular to the work as you near the end of each cut so the cutting depth is the same on both sides of the board. It often helps to hold the saw backward, as shown.

Using a power mitersaw

Most miters in deck construction are made from two pieces of wood cut at a 45-degree angle. Miter cuts must be precise. If they are off even 1 degree, the corner will have a noticeable gap.

The most inexpensive (and least accurate) way to make miter cuts is to use a wooden or plastic miter box—a jig that holds a backsaw at the proper angle to the workpiece. These miter boxes become inaccurate as the saw enlarges the guide slots. If you have many miter cuts to make, buy or rent a power mitersaw.

Power mitersaws are easy to set up, accurate, and safe. Some models have a few limitations, however. Standard power mitersaws won't cut compound miters easily; you'll need a compound mitersaw for that. A sliding compound mitersaw will make the cuts in wider stock.

Whenever possible start with a board that's longer than you need and make your miter cut first. Test it out and recut the miter if necessary. Then cut the other end of the piece to the proper length.

INSTALL A NEW BLADE

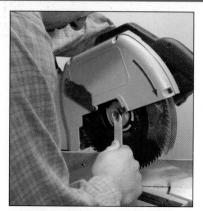

Unplug the saw and lock the blade with the locking mechanism. If your saw doesn't have one, lower the blade into a piece of scrap. Loosen and remove the arbor nut and blade. Mount the new blade and tighten the arbor nut securely.

1 Set angle on scale

To set the angle unlock the table (see the saw instructions) and move it to the desired setting.

2 Lock setting for cut

Once at the desired cut setting, lock the table in place. The saw instructions will tell you how to lock the table.

3 Unlock safety pin

Some manufacturers install a safety pin to keep the head locked down when the saw is not in use. The saw manual will tell you where to find the locking button and how to release it. You will need to release the button to operate the saw.

4 Make the cut

Set the work against the fence, start the saw, and lower it to the cutline.

OPERATE SAFELY

Mitersaws can be dangerous if used improperly. Follow these steps to ensure safe operation:

- Read the manufacturer's manual carefully. Make sure you fully understand the instructions before attempting to operate the saw. Ask the salesperson to demonstrate proper use.
- Wear safety glasses or a face shield for protection from flying wood chips. If the work produces a lot of dust, wear a dust mask.

- Power saws are noisy. Wear proper hearing protection while you work.
- Keep guards in place and in proper working order. Don't operate a saw without a guard.
- Wait for the motor to reach full speed before you begin cutting.
- Hold or clamp the workpiece against the table or fence. Never make freehand cuts.

Selecting lumber

Lumber used in deck construction must resist rot, so use pressure-treated or naturally resistant lumber.

Pressure-treated (PT) lumber, usually pine or fir, is infused with rot-resisting chemicals. It's the least expensive of your choices, but pick each board carefully so you get stock that is straight and free of loose knots.

Naturally resistant species, such as cedar, redwood, and cypress, resist rot and insects. But only the heartwood (the centermost core of the tree) is resistant. Seal or stain these woods to keep their natural beauty or let them weather to shades of gray. Exotic species such as ipe, cambara, and meranti are generally more durable but more difficult to work with and more expensive.

Unless your design requires the same wood throughout, use pressure-treated lumber for framing. For posts and framing within 6 inches of the soil, use boards rated for ground contact. Wood that has been kiln-dried after treatment (KDAT) is the highest quality.

Buy the best wood you can afford for decking and railings. Redwood, cedar, cypress, and the exotic species are good choices, but you should seal sapwoods.

Lumber is graded for its appearance, strength, and amount of knots. For structural members choose No. 2 grade or lumber graded as standard. For decking and railings select grades are free of knots but are expensive. Choose the best your budget will allow.

A lumber grade stamp (page 43) indicates the quality of the stock and its moisture content.

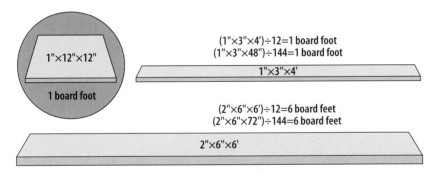

(1"×3"×4')÷12=1 board foot
(1"×3"×48")÷144=1 board foot
1"×3"×4'

(2"×6"×6')÷12=6 board feet
(2"×6"×72")÷144=6 board feet
2"×6"×6'

1"×12"×12"
1 board foot

The board foot

A board foot is a unit of measurement for lumber. To calculate the number of board feet in a board, multiply nominal width by nominal thickness in inches. Then multiply by the actual length in feet and divide by 12 or multiply by the length in inches and divide by 144.

SOME COMMON GRADES OF WOOD

Grade	Characteristics
Clear	Has no knots
Select or select structural	High-quality wood. Subdivided into Nos. 1–3 or grades A–D; the higher numbers and letters will have more knots
No. 2 common	Has tight knots, no major blemishes; good for shelving
No. 3 common	Some knots may be loose; often blemished or damaged
Construction or standard	Good strength; used for general framing
Utility	Economy grade used for rough framing

THE REAL SIZE OF LUMBER

Nominal lumber sizes state the dimensions before milling and drying. Actual sizes are smaller. Order lumber by its nominal size. When you measure it you measure its actual size.

Nominal	Actual
1×2	¾"×1½"
1×3	¾"×2½"
1×4	¾"×3½"
1×6	¾"×5½"
1×8	¾"×7¼"
1×10	¾"×9¼"
1×12	¾"×11¼"
2×2	1½"×1½"
2×4	1½"×3½"
2×6	1½"×5½"
2×8	1½"×7¼"
4×4	3½"×3½"
6×6	5½"×5½"

MIX AND MATCH

Different parts of a deck have different functions and visibility, so it isn't necessary to build the whole deck out of the same kind of wood. Unless you live on the West Coast where redwood may be cheap enough that you can use it for structural members, the best choice for posts, beams, and joists is usually pressure-treated lumber. By building the framing with less-expensive treated lumber, you can spend more on better-looking lumber for decking and railings.

Selecting lumber *(continued)*

LUMBER SELECTOR

Type		Description	Uses
Pressure-treated lumber		Softwood, tendency to be knotty. Resistant to rot, decay, and insects. Pronounced grain pattern that may raise when wet. Depending on chemical used, freshly treated stock has brown or greenish cast. Can be stained or painted. Weathers to a dull gray.	For framing, interior and exterior trim, shimming, stakes, latticework, and edging.
Cedar		Softwood, can be knotty, tends to split easily. Light pink to brown heartwood is less resistant to rot, decay, and insects than other resistant species but is more durable. Light-color sapwood is not resistant. Rich, light red natural color. Can be stained or painted. Weathers to an attractive gray.	For framing, decking, railings, paneling, trim, fascia, fencing, and outdoor furniture.
Redwood		Premium grade exterior wood, more resistant to rot, decay, and insect damage than cedar, but less than cypress. Vertical, even grain pattern, less susceptible to splitting than cedar. Light cherry red to deep red-brown. Can be stained or painted. Weathers quickly to an attractive gray.	For framing, decking, railings, paneling, trim, fascia, fencing, and outdoor furniture.
Cypress		Softwood, native to swampy regions of the southern United States. More rot-, decay-, and insect-resistant than other softwoods. Lightweight, very strong and durable. Straight grain pattern. Can be stained or painted. Weathers to a light gray.	For framing, decking, railings, paneling, trim, fascia, fencing, and outdoor furniture.
Ipe		Hardwood, very dense, extremely rot-resistant. Difficult to saw, plane, and drill. Requires carbide-tipped, high-quality tools. One of the most durable woods in outdoor applications. Deep brown-red to amber hues within the same board. Tight grain pattern, consistent from board to board. Difficult to finish, especially resistant to penetrating stains. Weathers to a pleasing gray. Predrilling for fasteners is required; stainless-steel fasteners recommended.	Expense makes use for framing prohibitive. For decking, railings, paneling, trim, and fascia.
Meranti		Hardwood, extremely resistant to decay and rot. Slightly less expensive than other tropical hardwoods. Interlocked, consistent grain pattern from board to board. Light red to dark red-brown. Can be finished with hardwood stains and exterior oils. Weathers to a rich gray. Predrilling is required. Stainless-steel fasteners recommended.	Expense makes use for framing prohibitive. For decking, railings, paneling, trim, and fascia.
Synthetics (composites, vinyl, fiberglass)		Materials manufactured from wood byproducts and resins, PVC, and fiberglass. Completely resistant to decay, rot, and insects. Easily cut and drilled, most are fastened with fasteners made for the material. Limited variety of appearances, but some wood-grain patterns are available in composite products.	Lightweight, not strong enough for framing. Most products made for decking, some for railings.

How much lumber will you need? For a small deck (10×12 feet, for example), the best way to calculate how much lumber you'll need is to draw a dimensioned plan and count all the pieces of each size—12-foot 2×4s and so forth. Add 10 percent to framing quantities and 15 percent to decking to allow for waste so you'll get everything you need.

For larger decks count framing members and estimate decking based on square footage.

HEARTWOOD OR SAPWOOD?

Light-color sapwood is less rot-resistant than the darker heartwood. Most lumber has both.

GRADE STAMPS

Grade stamps vary. All show wood species, grade, and grading agency. The stamp on pressure-treated lumber shows treatment information as well.

MANAGED FORESTS

Concerned that your lumber may come from irreplaceable forests? Several organizations monitor the forestry industry and promote responsible forest management. For information visit sustainable.org/economy/forestry.html.

HANDLING TREATED WOOD

Pressure-treated lumber is saturated with chemical preservatives, embedded in the wood's fibers. The industry says that when properly handled, pressure-treated wood is safe and the chemicals will not leach out of the wood. New chemicals are now in use, but existing stock of wood treated with chromated copper arsenate (CCA) can still be sold. When working with pressure-treated lumber, observe the following precautions:

- Wear work gloves (except when using power tools).
- Wear a dust mask and goggles when cutting.
- Wash hands before eating, drinking, or smoking.
- Never burn the wood or scraps.
- Dispose of wood scraps with regular trash.
- Don't use the wood indoors.
- Launder work clothes separately from other clothing, especially baby clothing and diapers.

INSPECT EACH BOARD BEFORE BUYING

If you order lumber by telephone, you will get someone else's choice of boards, not your own. Lumberyards usually have plenty of substandard wood lying around. The only way to be sure you do not get some of it is to pick out the boards yourself. Some lumberyards will not allow you to sort through the stacks because they want to keep wood neatly stacked—the only way to keep lumber from warping. But they should at least let you stand by and approve the selection. If not, make sure that you can return boards you don't want.

Twisted, bowed, some cupped boards, and boards with crooks can usually be brought into line when fastening (see page 85). Checks are not a structural problem, but don't buy split boards. Knots should be tight.

Twist

Bow

Cup

Crook

Knot

Check

Split

Calculating spans

To ensure that a deck is safe, strong, and durable, local building departments have strict codes regarding the sizes and types of posts, joists, footings, and beams. Many of these requirements relate to the distance each framing member can span without support.

The span limitations of any board depend on its quality, species, and the spacing of other framing members—and all are interrelated. For example, beam span for a deck with joists spaced 24 inches apart is different from the span allowed when the joists are spaced 16 inches apart.

When calculating allowable spans remember that specifications vary depending on the type of wood you use. Spans may also change for a deck that is higher than 12 feet.

The table at right shows spans typically allowed for pressure-treated Southern yellow pine. The specifications assume that the deck load is 50 pounds per square foot—10 pounds of dead load (the weight of the construction materials) and 40 pounds of live load (the weight of people and objects on the deck) per square foot.

Building codes vary. Contact your local building officials for advice when designing your deck.

Diagonal decking span

Joist span

Beam span

WOOD STRENGTH VARIES

Species and grades of wood vary in strength. Design your framing with the strength of the wood in mind. Southern yellow pine and Douglas fir have the same allowable spans and are the most common types of pressure-treated lumber. Redwood and Western red cedar require shorter spans.

DECK LUMBER SPANS

Beam Spans for Pressure-Treated Southern Yellow Pine
Maximum beam span between posts based on on-center distance between beams or ledger to beam

Nominal beam size	4'	5'	6'	7'	8'	9'	10'	11'	12'
(2) 2×6	7'	6'							
4×6	7'	7'	6'						
(2) 2×8	9'	8'	7'	7'	6'	6'			
4×8	10'	9'	8'	7'	7'	6'	6'	6'	
(2) 2×10	11'	10'	9'	8'	8'	7'	7'	6'	6'
(2) 2×12	13'	12'	10'	10'	9'	8'	8'	7'	7'

Joist Spans for Pressure-Treated Southern Yellow Pine
Maximum joist spans based on joist spacing

Nominal joist size	12" joist spacing	16" joist spacing	24" joist spacing
2×6	10' 4"	9' 5"	7' 10"
2×8	13' 8"	12' 5"	10' 2"
2×10	17' 5"	15' 5"	12' 7"

Decking Spans

Species	Nominal Decking Size	Recommended Span
Redwood, Western red cedar, and pressure-treated Southern yellow pine or Douglas fir	5/4×4, 5/4×6 radius-edge (except Southern yellow pine)	16"
	5/4×4, 5/4×6 radius-edge Southern yellow pine	24"
	2×4, 2×6	24"

Ordering and storing lumber

With your plans drawn, you can make a list of the lumber and other materials you'll need to complete your deck.

The list at the right shows most of what you'll need for a 12×20-foot deck, but because lumber is sold in even-numbered lengths, your final order could look different.

Plan your order for the most efficient use of the lumber you buy. For example, decking for the project at right requires two boards to complete each run. You could buy a 14-foot board and an 8-foot board to complete each run, but you'll have less waste if you buy all 14-footers and cut some of them in half.

A lumber and materials list will make it easier for you to shop around for the best price. But don't shop for price alone—compare delivery fees and be sure to find out whether you will be able to return unused lumber.

PLAN FOR OUTSIDE LUMBER STORAGE

Store wood outside by stacking it with 2×2 strips (stickers) between layers to create airspaces. Use concrete blocks or 4×4s to keep the stack off the ground. Weight the stack to help prevent warping and cover the stack with a tarp. If your lumber is not kiln-dried, let it dry for several weeks.

LUMBER AND MATERIALS LIST FOR A 12×20-FOOT PLATFORM DECK

Foundation (for 3-foot frost line)	Quantity	Material/Size
Premix concrete (cubic feet)	$4\frac{2}{3}$	
Fiber tube forms	4	8×38"
Gravel or sand for drainage	as needed	
Rebar	8	No. 4 L-shape pieces
Framing		
Ledger board	1	2×8×10'
	1	2×8×9'9"
Metal flashing	as needed	as needed
Posts	4	4×4×height shown on plan
Beams	2	2×10×13'
	2	2×10×7'
Plywood spacers (for beams)	11	$\frac{1}{2}$×3×8"
Joists	16	2×8×11'9"
End joists	2	2×8×12'
Header joist	1	2×8×6'6"
	1	2×8×13'3"
Decking		
Decking boards	39	2×6×14'
Nails and fasteners		
Joist hangers	12	2×8
	2	$3\frac{1}{2}$×8
Post anchors	4	4×4
Post caps	4	4×4
Bolts or anchors for ledger		as needed
16d common nails or 3-inch decking screws @1,000/lb.		about 14 pounds
Optional		
Stairs		as required by plan
Railings		as required by plan
Sealer/stain		see pages 126–129

Ready-made railings

Railing style can enhance the appearance of your deck more than anything else. Square-cut post and baluster styles are the most common and will complement almost any architectural style. Dress them up with mortises, bevel cuts, and post caps.

You can use the stock material at your home center and add decorative chamfers, angles, or dadoes with your tablesaw or mitersaw. If you want something different and more stylish than rectangular railing stock, look at the supply of milled railing materials at your home center.

There are many styles in different species. Turned balusters are available in many shapes and sizes and go well with Victorian or classic landscape designs. Infill can be all the same style milled balusters in each panel or a mix of various baluster styles with a consistent post design for more variety.

Milled stock is more expensive, of course. Save some expense by cutting straight balusters for alternate railing panels and inserting turned stock in the panels in between.

Finials and post caps will also add distinct style to your posts. Finials come in a bountiful number of shapes to fit 4×4 or 6×6 posts. Some come complete with lag screws that only require predrilling the posts. Other styles have to be mounted with screws or dowels. To keep rainwater from settling in under the finial and rotting the top of the post, caulk the bottom edge with silicone before tightening the finial.

Post caps cover the top of the posts completely and shed rain from the end grain. You'll find them fluted, corniced, and chamfered—in styles that will match any deck design.

Designing with posts

Prefabricated posts add flexibility to your deck design. They're made in all materials—even vinyls and synthetics. Don't finalize your railing design until you know what's out there. If you can't find what you want on your home center racks, ask for a catalog; there may be others you can order.

Alternatives to wood

Manufacturers of vinyl and wood-resin composites offer some railing components. They look best when the entire railing is made of the same materials. Consider steel or anodized aluminum also. The right metal design can add a style to your railing not otherwise possible.

Post caps and finials

Some home centers and specialty lumberyards carry turned post finials and a variety of wood, metal, and plastic post caps. Other suppliers advertise in home improvement or landscaping publications, and you'll find many sell their products on the Internet.

Designing with balusters

Square-cut balusters will go with almost any architectural style. Turned balusters won't. Balusters with a few flutes and collars fit into restrained neoclassical themes. Elaborate turnings look best in Victorian settings.

Choosing fasteners

Whether you use screws or nails to hold your deck together, they (and the anchoring hardware) must withstand years of moisture and the stress of normal use.

When you choose fasteners you'll have as many choices as you do choosing other materials. Standard galvanized fasteners have a single protective coating, and that coating may flake off allowing the fastener to rust. Rust not only weakens the fastener, it stains the wood. Double-dipped galvanized fasteners are better, but you'll get the longest life and best appearance from coated fasteners made for decks.

Nails

Nails are indirectly sized by their length. Each length is expressed as a penny size, such as 16-penny or 16d. (The d stands for "denarius," the Roman penny. Some say the size referred to the price of 100 nails of a size—16 pennies for larger ones, 6 pennies for smaller ones, for instance.) Choose nails by length; see "The Right Nail for the Job."

Common nails used for general framing have large heads and thick shanks. They hold well but may split the wood. Box nails are thinner and reduce splitting.

Ringshank and spiral nails grip the wood fibers and don't easily work their way out, which is good for fastening decking. They are difficult to pull out.

Finishing nails are good where you don't want the nailhead to show. Use them to fasten fascia and cap rails. After driving them drive the heads below the surface with a nail set, then fill the holes.

Screws

There are many kinds of screws. Buy #10 deck screws in 2½- to 3½-inch lengths. Deck screws are coated to resist the elements. They're sharp and tapered (for easy driving), and the heads countersink themselves. With a cordless drill you can drive them about as fast as nails. Deck screws come with a phillips, square, or combination head. To drive square or combination heads without slipping, chuck a square-tip screwdriver bit in your drill.

Framing hardware

Building codes require framing hardware for many connections. These connectors strengthen the joints. Attach joists to beams with joist hangers. At the corners use angle brackets.

Where a beam sits on a post, a post/beam connector provides a secure connection. On beams some codes require seismic ties with joists to add lateral strength.

A post anchor secures a post to a concrete pier and supports it above grade so the bottom won't sit in a puddle. Get adjustable post anchors so you can line up the post centers.

THE RIGHT NAIL FOR THE JOB

Use nails three times as long as the thickness of the material you are fastening. To attach a 1×4 board (¾ inch thick), a 6d finishing nail that's 2 inches long will be a bit short. An 8d nail is 2½ inches long, a little more than three times the thickness of the 1×4, so it will do better. Make sure the nail will not go through the other side of the material you are nailing to.

Equivalent sizes of some nails:

3d=1¼"	10d=3"
4d=1½"	12d=3¼"
6d=2"	16d=3½"
7d=2¼"	20d=4"
8d=2½"	

16d galvanized box nails   3" coated deck screws   12d ringshank nails

12d spiral nails   10d galvanized casing nails   10d galvanized box nails

8d galvanized siding nails   6d galvanized siding nails   ³/₁₆"×3¼" masonry screws

Choosing fasteners *(continued)*

Heavy-duty screws and bolts

To fasten large framing members, such as railing posts to joists, use lag screws, machine bolts, or carriage bolts. Bolts are stronger and can be tightened in the future if the lumber shrinks. Always use washers under the head of a lag screw or machine bolt and the nut on a carriage or machine bolt so that the fastener does not sink into the wood.

To attach wood to brick, block, or concrete, use lag screws and lag shields. To tack a ledger temporarily, use masonry screws; they're not as strong but are much easier to drive and don't require an anchor.

J-bolt

Lag screw with masonry anchor

Carriage bolt

Lag screw

LIQUID FASTENERS

Many carpentry jobs call for adhesives, either as the primary or secondary fastener. Purchase several tubes of construction adhesive to help keep miters from separating. Two-part epoxy in syringes is self-mixing. You'll need it to anchor threaded studs in post footings.

Hidden clips and rails

Various hardware allows you to install decking without any visible fasteners. Deck clips, recessed fasteners, and metal rails attach the decking to the joists, either between or under the decking. For information about installing these fasteners, see page 87.

Seismic /hurricane tie

Joist hanger

Angled joist hanger

Nonadjustable post anchor

Corner bracket

Joist connector

Adjustable post anchor

Post/beam connector

Footings and flashing

Deck footings support the entire load of the structure. Footings usually consist of round holes in the ground that extend below the frost line and are filled with concrete. Different building codes, climates, and soil conditions may call for different footings. Precast piers set in concrete or tamped earth are one example (below). The type and dimensions of your deck footings will ultimately depend on the height of the deck, the types of materials you use, how deep the ground freezes, and the load-bearing capacity of the soil.

Most building codes require that a deck support a dead load (weight of materials) of 10 pounds per square foot and a live load (weight of people and furnishings) of 40 pounds per square foot, or a total of 50 pounds per square foot. All the framing works together—the ledger carries a portion of the weight, which it transfers to the foundation of the house; beams carry the intermediate loads, and footings

support the loads that are transferred to the perimeter.

Preventing frost heave

In cold climates soil freezes and thaws, causing the soil to expand and contract—movement that can break up the deck if footings are not set properly. In different regions the ground freezes to different depths during the winter. Footings have to be dug below this frost line. Local codes will specify the frost line and how far below it you must set your footings.

In warm climates you may only need a shallow footing—about 6 to 12 inches deep and 1 to 2 feet square. Even in some winter climates, codes allow you to set posts in a tamped earth footing.

Soils and slopes

Loose soils have less load-bearing capacity and may require more or larger footings than heavy clay or compacted soils. Posts set in sloping terrain should have at least 7 feet of soil horizontally

between the bottom of the footing and the surface of the slope.

Considering all of these variations, don't be surprised if you find that your codes specify different spacings or construction methods than are noted in standard span tables.

Estimating concrete

Concrete volume is stated in cubic yards. To estimate the quantity, use this formula: 3.14 (pi) × the radius of the hole (in feet) squared × depth (in feet), divided by 27.

Thus the volume of a hole 1 foot in diameter (½-foot radius) and 3½ feet deep would be (3.14 × .25 × 3.5)/27 or .10 cubic yard. That doesn't seem like much, but for 12 footings it would be more than a cubic yard. Two 60-pound bags of premix should fill one 3-foot hole. Order ready-mix truck delivery whenever you need a cubic yard of concrete or more.

Use precast piers

Precast concrete piers are available at home centers. They may be used with or without footings, depending on local code requirements. They may be used without hardware, as shown above, to simplify construction of ground-level decks.

When using a precast pier to support a post, install a post anchor in the center or purchase piers that have the hardware already mounted, as shown above.

Use fiber tube forms

Fiber tube forms make it easy to cast footings and may be required by code in areas with loose or sandy soils. Sold in various lengths and widths, the tubes should be cut as squarely as possible with a handsaw, then suspended above the bottom of the hole (see page 63) to allow concrete to spread out and form a flared base.

Footings and flashing *(continued)*

Reinforce with rebar

Reinforcing steel bars, or rebar, add strength to concrete structures and in some areas may be required. If rebar is needed building codes will specify how many and what size. Deck footings typically need one or two lengths of rebar set in the concrete.

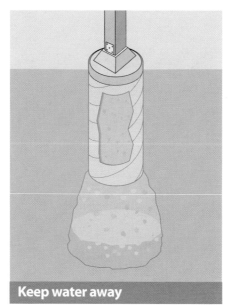

Keep water away

Water can pool around the bottom of a post, leading to rot. Improve a footing by shaping the top to drain moisture away from the post base. On a flat-top footing, install an elevated or standoff post base.

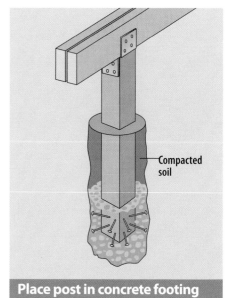

Compacted soil

Place post in concrete footing

This foundation uses only a small amount of concrete to form a footing entirely below the frost line. The post must be rated for ground contact. Drive nails into each side to hold the post in the concrete. Backfill the remainder of the hole with compacted layers of soil.

Mix your own concrete

You can mix your own concrete for footings. If you have more than six or eight footings to pour, mixing your own can be more cost-effective than buying premixed bags.

Shovel the dry ingredients into a wheelbarrow or power mixer—1 part portland cement, $2\frac{1}{4}$ parts sand, $2\frac{1}{2}$ to 3 parts gravel. Mix the dry ingredients together first, then add water a little at a time and mix again. Keep adding water until the concrete clings to a shovel turned on edge.

Flashing

Flashing comes preformed in Z-shape sections, in rolls, or as a self-stick synthetic membrane. Flashing keeps water from collecting behind the ledger and rotting both it and the house framing. Purchase whatever style you find convenient.

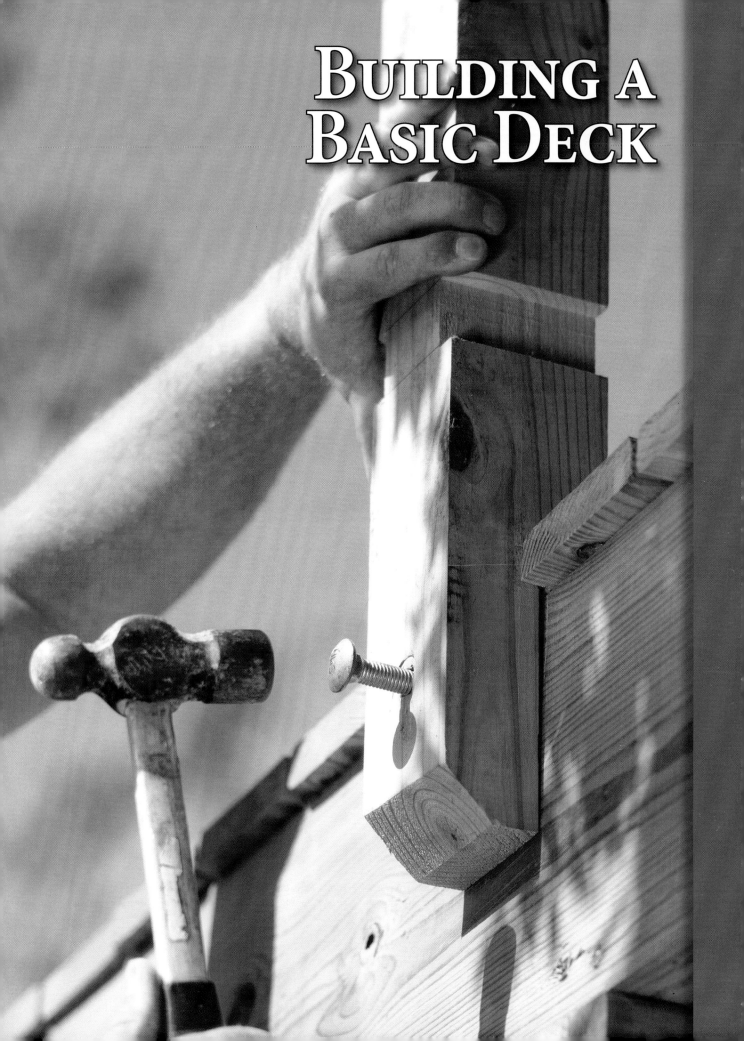

BUILDING A BASIC DECK

Installing a ledger on siding

- **TIME:** 4 to 5 hours for a 16-foot ledger
- **SKILLS:** Cutting, drilling, driving fasteners
- **TOOLS:** Hammer, chalkline, tape measure, water level, drill, layout square, circular saw, chisel, caulking gun, socket wrench, snips

I f your deck will be attached to your house, installing a ledger is the first step in laying out the site. (Freestanding decks are supported on all sides by posts and footings.)

A ledger is a header that's attached to the house. It transfers the weight of the deck to the framing and foundation of the house. That's why the fasteners on a frame house (usually lag screws but sometimes bolts) must penetrate the sheathing and anchor firmly into the band joist or studs. On brick, block, or concrete construction, use masonry anchors or studs in holes drilled into the masonry.

Installing a ledger usually requires removing the siding so the ledger can rest against a flat surface. Cut metal siding with a circular saw and a metal-cutting blade. Cut vinyl and wood siding with a circular saw and a carbide-tipped blade.

Be careful when cutting your ledger. Use the same size stock as the joists. Cut the ledger 3 inches shorter than the width of the framing to allow a 1½-inch space at each end of the ledger for attaching the rim joists.

Using a ledger can reduce your costs and labor—you have fewer postholes to dig and less concrete to pour.

Locate the ledger on the house

The framing and foundation of your house provide several secure points for anchoring the ledger. The actual placement of the ledger will depend on your deck design and the location of the door that provides access to it. Most decks are first-floor structures and anchor into the band joist. Other deck designs will require that you drive the fasteners into the studs or into the masonry foundation.

Ledger on siding

Wherever you put the ledger—if your house is sided with wood, metal, or vinyl siding—a section of the siding has to come off. Installing the ledger on top of the siding will crush the siding, leaving the ledger in incomplete contact with the surface behind it. That could cause the ledger to fail. Ledgers also need flashing (preformed or flat metal stock), which slides under the siding and extends over the ledger to keep water from collecting behind it.

1 Mark the top edge of the ledger

Decking should sit from 1 to 3 inches below the bottom of the threshold. Add this space to the thickness of the decking and make a mark for the top of the ledger. For 5/4×6 decking with the surface 3 inches below the door, your mark would fall 4¼ inches below the bottom of the threshold.

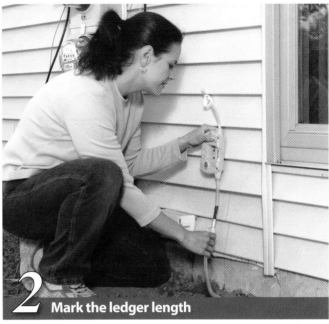

2 Mark the ledger length

Set one end of a water level on your mark and the other at a point longer than the length of the ledger. Mark one side then the other with the same method. Snap a chalkline between the marks. Add 1½ inches to the length of the ledger and mark this length on your chalkline.

3 Check for level

At both ends of the ledger marks, measure down from the top line an amount equal to the width of the ledger. Snap chalklines between the marks or use a level or straightedge to connect the marks on short ledgers. Check your lines for level at various points and adjust them if necessary.

LAG SCREWS OR BOLTS

You can bolt the ledger to the band joist, but you need to reach the back to put on the nut. Lag screws are easier to install and make a strong connection. Use carriage bolts for bolted joints when the head will be visible and hex-head machine bolts when looks don't matter.

CAUTION

LEDGERS AND LADDERS

Installing a ledger for a first-floor deck won't pose a serious safety problem. But for a second-story deck, you will have to work on a ladder. Ledgers can be heavy and throw you off balance. Use braces (page 54) or get some help. Drive stakes against the bottom of the ladder legs to keep the ladder from slipping on a slope.

Installing a ledger on siding *(continued)*

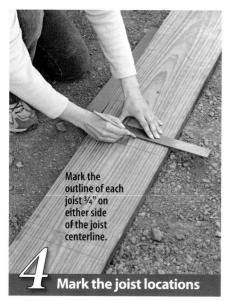

Mark the outline of each joist ¾" on either side of the joist centerline.

4 Mark the joist locations

Mark the joist spacing (16 or 24 inches center-to-center) on the ledger, allowing for the rim joists to be attached to the ends of the ledger. For 16-inch centers make the mark for the edge of the first interior joist 15¼ inches from the end of the ledger. Transfer the marks to the ledger face.

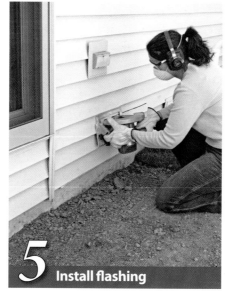

5 Install flashing

Set your circular saw depth to the thickness of the siding and cut along the ledger outline. Cut flashing to the length of the cutout and slide it at least 1 inch under the siding above the cutout. Pressure will hold it in place. Overlap flashing joints by 3 inches and notch it for the doorway.

6 Level the ledger

Hoist the ledger into place and center it in the cutout, leaving 1½ inches on either side for the rim joists. Tack one end of the ledger to the sheathing with one 10d nail or deck screw. Level the ledger and tack the other end. Don't fasten it just yet.

FINISHING THE CUTS

A circular saw can't cut into the corners on the siding. Chisel out the corners on wood siding with a sharp wood chisel. Cut metal and vinyl siding corners with metal snips.

USE BRACES WHEN WORKING ALONE

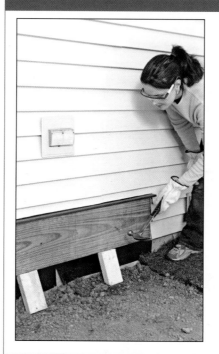

If you're working by yourself, putting the ledger into its exact position and getting it to stay there can be almost impossible unless you use braces.

Cut 2×4 braces a little longer than the height of the ledger and notch one end if you want. Prop the braces at an angle below both ends of the ledger cutout. Then lift the ledger and set it on the braces—one at a time, if necessary.

Keeping the face of the ledger flat against the sheathing, slide the ledger so it's centered in the opening, leaving 1½ inches on each end for the rim joists. Adjust the brace on one end with one hand (don't let go of the ledger) until the top of the ledger rests on the top of the cutout. Tack this end to the sheathing with a 10d nail or deck screw. Pivot the ledger on this fastener, level the board by adjusting the brace at the other end of the ledger, and tack that end of the ledger.

For ledgers fastened to studs, space fasteners at house stud spacing.

Keep fasteners about 2 inches from top and bottom edge.

7 Mark for fasteners

Beginning about 2 inches from one end, mark fastener locations at 18- to 24-inch intervals. Mark both the top and bottom edge of the ledger, using a layout square. Don't worry if a fastener is at a deck joist location.

8 Drill pilot holes

Drill pilot holes for the lag screws through the ledger and about ¾ inch into the band joist or studs. Counterbore for lag-screws that fall on deck joist markings. Drive washered lag screws with a socket wrench.

9 Seal the edges

Let the ledger settle overnight, then tighten the screws again, stopping when they won't turn without force. Caulk the counterbores, the top of the flashing, and the bottom of the ledger with exterior silicone caulk.

Installing a ledger on stucco

Kerf in stucco

Ledger installed over stucco

Flashing

Lag screws anchored in band joist or studs

Stucco siding

Stucco acts essentially as a layer of siding (one that consists of concrete), so fastening a ledger to stucco involves the same techniques as for wood or vinyl siding. Stucco doesn't have to be removed but does require a groove for anchoring the flashing.

1 Cut a groove

Hang the ledger on the stucco. Mark the wall about an inch above the ledger and tack a guide on the ledger so the saw blade will cut on the mark. Using a circular saw with a masonry blade, cut a ¼-inch-deep kerf from one end of the ledger to the other.

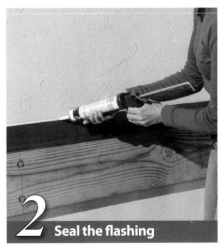

2 Seal the flashing

Blow the dust out of the kerf with a compressed-air can, then push the lip of the flashing into the kerf until it's seated firmly. Seal the top of the flashing with silicone caulk.

Installing a ledger on masonry

- **TIME:** 4 to 5 hours for a 16-foot ledger
- **SKILLS:** Cutting, drilling, driving fasteners
- **TOOLS:** Hammer, chalkline, tape measure, water level, drill, layout square, circular saw, chisel, caulking gun, socket wrench, masonry bit

A ledger on a brick, block, or poured concrete wall has to be anchored to the masonry material because there's no framing to support it. It must be securely fastened so it can withstand the downward pressure of the deck.

The beam and perimeter posts bear about half of the load of the deck away from the house. The ledger must support the rest of the weight.

You can secure the ledger to the masonry with epoxied threaded studs (as shown at right) or lag shields and lag screws. If you epoxy-glue threaded studs into the masonry, use epoxy made for that purpose. Lag shields are made to be used with lag screws. Don't use any other masonry anchor. Although most of the stress put on ledger anchors will be down (not out), inadequate anchors could let the deck work loose and pull away from the wall.

Ledger on masonry

There are two kinds of threaded studs: short precut lengths for use in masonry installations and continuous threaded lengths (up to 4 feet) called all-thread. Cutting all-thread to length often results in damaged or distorted threads and uneven lengths. Precut studs are easier to use. Use studs with a diameter of at least ⅜ inch; ½-inch studs are better. When fastening a ledger to concrete block, be sure the fasteners enter the webs (the solid part) of the block, not the cores (the open voids).

Silicone caulk

Flashing

Ledger

Threaded studs, lag shields and lag screws, or anchor bolts

1 Outline the ledger

Mark the wall so the top edge of the ledger will be at the correct point below the threshold. For short ledgers extend the mark along the wall with a carpenter's level. Use a water level or laser level for long spans. Mark the length of the ledger and snap a line between the marks.

2 Tack the ledger in place

Mark the ledger for both joist and fastener locations. Then tack the ledger to the masonry with concrete screws, making sure the ledger is level with your chalkline. Brace the ledger against the wall if necessary.

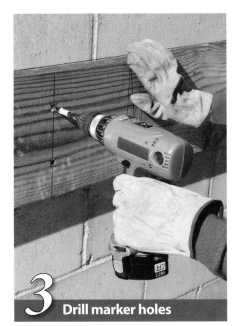

3 Drill marker holes

Mark a twist drill just short of 1½ inches and drill marker holes at your fastener locations. Don't push past the mark on the drill bit or you'll ruin the tip of the twist drill against the masonry.

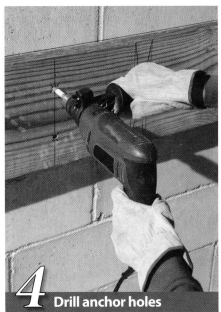

4 Drill anchor holes

Insert a masonry bit of the same size in a hammer drill and drill the fastener holes 3 inches into the masonry. The hammer drill will push through the undrilled wood at the bottom of the marker hole.

5 Epoxy the holes

Remove the ledger if you prefer. Prepare the epoxy syringe, making sure both its parts will mix evenly. Insert the syringe in the hole and push out the epoxy—only into the masonry, not the ledger.

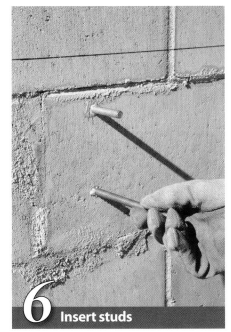

6 Insert studs

Insert a threaded stud into each hole right after you've epoxied it. If you wait until all the holes are epoxied, the glue may set up, so you might not be able to get the studs into the first holes. Square the studs to the ledger (or to the wall if you've removed the ledger) with a layout square.

7 Install washers and nuts

Let the epoxy cure overnight and replace the ledger over the studs if you previously removed it. Slide washers over the studs and tighten the nuts with a socket wrench. Don't overtighten—stop when the washer begins to dent the wood.

USING LAG SCREWS

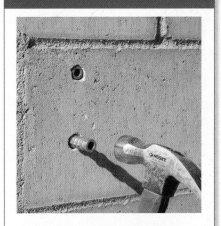

To fasten the ledger with lag screws, install lag shields. Tack (or brace) the ledger in place and drill marker holes, then mark the wall with a small masonry bit. Remove the ledger and use a larger masonry bit to drill holes for the lag shields. Tap the shields flush with the wall and attach the ledger with the lag screws.

Preparing the site

- ■ **TIME:** About 1 hour to run lines; more to remove sod and lay fabric
- ■ **SKILLS:** Measuring, digging
- ■ **TOOLS:** Spade, rake, hammer, small sledgehammer, mason's line

Most deck sites require some preparation so the ground under the deck will drain properly and won't become filled with weeds. You can prepare the site after laying out the batterboards, but removing the sod first will make the layout easier.

Eliminate any drainage problems, especially around the foundation.

Beginning at the foundation and out to about 4 feet, slope the soil away from the house. If a downspout empties on the deck site, reroute it. Divert water that will flow off the deck with a drainage ditch around the perimeter.

1 Stake the corners

Drive a temporary stake (or a batterboard) near the house about where the corner of the deck will be (or just outside the corner). Using your scaled plan, measure and stake the other three corners. You don't need to be exact; you'll fine-tune the outline later.

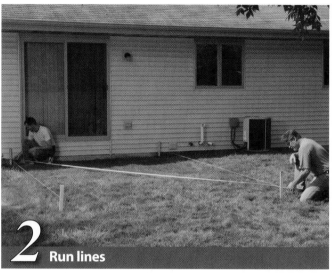

2 Run lines

Run mason's line between the stakes a couple of inches above the ground. Measure the diagonals and adjust the stakes until the diagonals are equal. Tighten the lines and spray paint or chalk the footprint on the grass.

3 Remove the sod and soil

Remove the lines and slice the sod in strips with a spade. Dislodge the roots with a spade and roll up the sod. Leave the stakes in place. Excavate the site to a 2-inch depth.

Lay gravel before or after digging postholes.

4 Lay fabric and gravel

Lay landscape fabric (weed block) in the excavation from edge to edge, overlapping the seams by 6 to 12 inches. Pour in crushed stone and rake it level with a garden rake.

Laying out a deck

■ **TIME:** About 6 hours for a 12×16-foot deck
■ **SKILLS:** Measuring, leveling, making simple calculations
■ **TOOLS:** Tape measure, cordless drill, sledgehammer, plumb bob, mason's line, line level

Laying out a deck site—marking the perimeter of the deck with mason's lines and locating the footings—isn't hard work, but it does require some precision. It doesn't have to be perfect because you can still make minor adjustments when you set the posts, but the success of your project depends on aligning the centers of the footings. Although laying out the site won't wear you out, you can do it much more quickly and accurately with someone to help pull lines tight, hold the loose end of the measuring tape, adjust lines, and double-check the layout for errors.

You'll need a pair of batterboards (page 60) at each corner. If you can't drive them close to the house, substitute a stake or 1× board tacked to the siding. Mason's lines tied to batterboards allow

you to square the corners and provide straight lines for centering the footings for the posts between the corners.

The illustration below shows a typical site layout and its relationship to the finished deck. All mason's lines run through the center of the footings. Pages 60–61 illustrate layout steps for a freestanding deck. If you've already fastened a ledger to the house for an attached deck, start with the steps for "Laying out with a ledger" on page 61, then follow the remaining steps to complete your layout.

After laying out the deck, set up a worksite close by, but out of the way.

Before you dig postholes check with the utility companies to have underground lines in the area marked.

Ledger

Stake or batterboard

Beam

Posts (will be attached to footings or piers)

Footing

Mason's lines mark centers of posts.

Keep mason's lines level.

Batterboards (2 to 3 feet beyond temporary stakes)

Laying out a deck *(continued)*

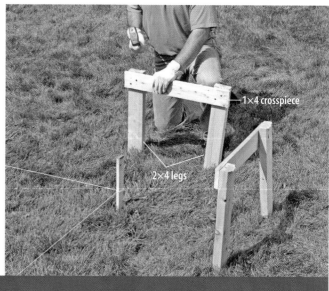

1×4 crosspiece

2×4 legs

1 Build batterboards

Make batterboards from 2- to 3-foot pointed 2×4 legs and an 18- to 36-inch 1×4 crosspiece. You might need batterboards with longer legs on a sloped site. Many lumberyards and home centers sell pointed stakes, or you can cut points on the stakes yourself. Cut the crosspiece to length and attach it to the stakes with 1½-inch screws. Place the batterboards at right angles to each other and 2 to 3 feet beyond your temporary corner stakes. If you use a stake at the house, center it in line with the center of your corner post. Drive the stakes deep enough to support tightly stretched lines. The crosspieces should be about 18 to 24 inches above grade.

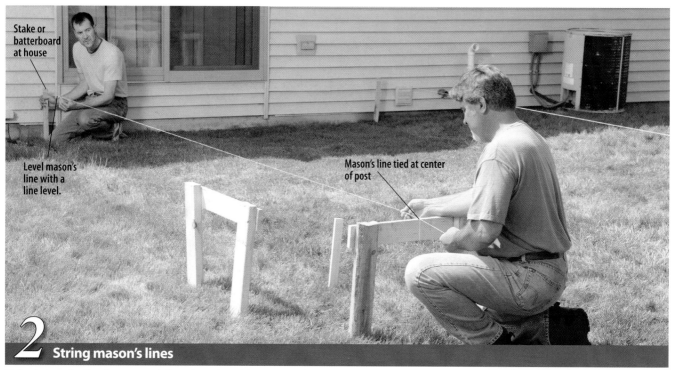

Stake or batterboard at house

Level mason's line with a line level.

Mason's line tied at center of post

2 String mason's lines

Stringing and adjusting mason's lines is easier with two people. Mark the siding for the edge of the decking, then for the center of the corner post. The post is usually placed inside the decking line a distance equal to the amount of overhang plus the thickness of the rim joist plus half the thickness of the post. Tie a line to the crosspiece (or stake) at this point and to the crosspiece of the corner batterboard. Keep it roughly square to the house. Do the same on the opposite side of the deck. Next, tie a mason's line parallel to the house and lined up with the center of the footings. Pull the lines tight and level them by driving in the batterboards. Make sure the lines touch where they intersect.

3 Square the layout

To square the layout use any even multiple of a 3-4-5 triangle. The larger the numbers, the greater the accuracy. In this case measure 6 feet along one line and mark the spot with a piece of tape. Measure 8 feet along the perpendicular line or on the siding and mark it also. Measure the distance between the two marks. If it is exactly 10 feet, the lines are square. If not, adjust one line. Square each corner with the same method.

4 Mark the crosspiece

Once you've squared the layout, mark the position of the line on each crosspiece. If the lines get bumped or when you need to take them down and restring them, you can reset them to the marks to maintain the layout.

5 Mark the footings

To mark the center of a corner footing, hold a plumb line barely touching the intersection of the lines. Drive a stake or landscape spike into the ground to mark the spot below the plumb bob. If your design includes line posts between the corners, measure along the line and use a plumb bob to mark the center of the footings. Mark an X across each stake or spike with chalk or spray paint.

Laying out with a ledger

Mason's line tied at center of post

Batterboard or 1×4 tacked to the siding

1 Plumb the corner

Drive a nail into the ledger at the centerline of the post (Step 2, opposite page). Drop a plumb line from the nail to the batterboard (or 1×4).

2 Tie line to batterboard

Let the plumb bob come to rest. Hold a scrap 1× just touching the plumb line and mark the crosspiece where the scrap intersects it. Tie a mason's line at this mark and continue your layout, following the procedure that begins in Step 2 on the opposite page.

Digging footings

- **TIME:** 1 to 4 hours, depending on the digging tool, the type of soil, and number and depth of the holes
- **SKILLS:** Using a manual posthole digger requires no special skills, but get instructions before using a power auger
- **TOOLS:** Shovel, clamshell posthole digger, digging bar, plywood or plastic sheet, level, handsaw, small sledgehammer, tamper

Before you dig footings check with your local building department for specific requirements for type, depth, and strength of posts and footings. Footings need to be stable in soft soil, withstand frost, and provide a base that keeps posts or beams above moisture. See page 49 for more information on footing options. Also have utility companies survey the area to locate and mark underground lines.

In cold climates footings should extend below the frost line (the depth to which frost penetrates the soil). This prevents the deck structure from rising and falling during freeze-thaw cycles.

Frost depth is not the only thing that affects the depth of the footing. Soil composition, the size of the post, and the height of the deck also affect footing depth.

Don't dig postholes with a shovel; borrow, rent, or buy a clamshell digger. A clamshell digger is an efficient tool for digging a few holes by hand, better than the old-style hand auger. If your design requires a number of footings, rent a power auger (see page 28) or hire a professional. If you rent a power auger, be sure to get instructions on its use. If you will pile soil on a grassy area, lay a sheet of plywood or plastic first.

A typical footing

2" above grade

Plumb and level form.

2×4 staked braces

Rebar (if required)

Concrete tube form

Gravel base

A typical footing installation consists of a concrete tube form set in the hole and plumbed with braced stakes. The hole will probably be a little larger than the tube form, so be sure to center the form before you stake the braces. If codes require rebar don't put it in the center of the hole— that's where the J-bolt goes.

CAUTION

WATCH YOUR BACK

Digging postholes is hard work. It could take a couple of hours to dig one posthole 3 to 4 feet deep. You may spend a lot of this time prying out rocks and cutting through roots. Don't try to grind out rocks with a clamshell digger. Pry them from the sides of the hole with a tamper.

Digging postholes can be tough on your arms and shoulders and tougher on your back. Even if you are in relatively good physical shape, take your time and take frequent breaks.

1 Start the footing

Unstring the mason's lines and spread your feet on both sides of the X that marks the center of the footing. With the handles of the digger parallel to each other, drive the blades into the soil. Let the weight of the digger do as much of the work as possible.

2 Remove the soil

Pull the handles apart to hold the soil between the blades and lift the digger straight up. Move the digger away from the hole and release the soil by pushing the handles together. At the proper depth flare the bottom of the hole by angling the blades.

3   Pour a gravel base

Clean out loose soil from the bottom of the hole and pour in 2 to 6 inches of crushed gravel (or the depth required by code). Tamp the gravel with a 2×4 or tamping bar. The gravel lets water drain out the bottom of the footing and helps reduce frost heave.

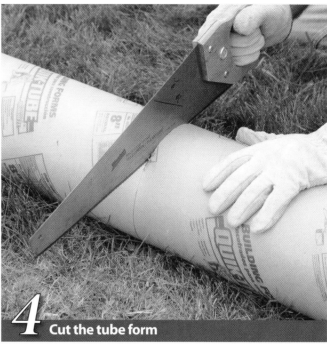

4   Cut the tube form

Mark the tube form so it will reach the level where the hole flares and extend 2 inches above grade. Cut the form with a handsaw, keeping the saw perpendicular to the form to make a straight cut. If the cut looks awkward, put that end in the bottom of the hole. A straight cut, however, makes the form easier to level.

5   Brace the form

Place the form in the hole and fasten it to 2× braces with screws. Drive stakes at both ends of the braces. Fasten one end of each brace to a stake and set a 2-foot level on the form. Raise or lower the brace to level the tube, then screw the braces to the stakes. Set the form as plumb as possible (it doesn't have to be perfect).

6   Backfill the form

Backfill the outside edge of the form with a round-nose shovel, tamping the soil lightly with a 2×2 after every 4 inches of soil. If the footing hole is more than 3 inches wider than the tube, tamping may fill the flared recess at the bottom of the hole. In this case pour the footing first, then backfill.

Pouring footings

■ **TIME:** About 1 hour per footing
■ **SKILLS:** Basic masonry skills; follow instructions on the bag to mix concrete
■ **TOOLS:** Power mixer or wheelbarrow, mason's hoe, shovel, mason's line, plumb bob or tape measure, layout square, trowel

If your deck will have corner footings only, preparing premixed bags of concrete in a wheelbarrow is quick and cost-effective. If you're pouring more than six footings, rent a power mixer or order truck-delivered ready-mix from a concrete supplier.

Either move the mixer to each hole or move the concrete in a wheelbarrow. Lay a 2×12 ramp to make the job easier and minimize damage to your lawn. Measure the dry ingredients first (in shovelfuls), mix them in the power mixer or wheelbarrow, then add the water.

Post base with nonadjustable anchor

Adjustable post anchor

Anchor base

J-bolt

Post-anchor options

Post anchors are made in a number of styles, either adjustable or nonadjustable. Nonadjustable anchors are slightly less expensive but require precise setting. Adjustable anchors will give you a margin of error, allowing a correction of up to 1/2 inch, which makes them worth their slightly higher cost. It's a lot easier to adjust an anchor to center the posts than it is to set the anchor precisely. The installation of footings shown on pages 65–66 involves inserting a J-bolt, which is anchored in the concrete and accepts an adjustable anchor.

MIXING IN A WHEELBARROW

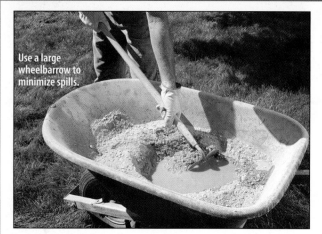

Use a large wheelbarrow to minimize spills.

Pour in a whole bag of premix (never a partial one) or measure dry ingredients in shovelfuls. Mix the ingredients with a hoe, then mound them and make a depression. Add water in the depression and pull the dry mix into the water, working the mix back and forth and scraping up dry material from the bottom. Add water as necessary.

GETTING THE RIGHT MIX

Whether you're mixing in a wheelbarrow or in a power mixer, make sure all of the ingredients are mixed together thoroughly. To test the consistency of the mix (its slump), scoop up some with a shovel or trowel. When the concrete clings to a shovel or a trowel turned on edge, it's ready.

1 Mix the dry ingredients

Bring the mixer or wheelbarrow to the hole. Empty whole premix bags into the mixer or measure cement, sand, and aggregate in shovelfuls. Turn the mixer on to mix the dry materials thoroughly. Then add half the water and mix again. Continue mixing, adding water a little at a time.

2 Make the pour

Tip the mixer or wheelbarrow so the concrete pours straight into the hole. Have a helper guide the flow with a round-nose shovel. Stop pouring when the hole is half full and consolidate the concrete (see Step 3), then fill the hole.

3 Consolidate the mix

When the footing is half full (and again when full), consolidate the mix by working a board up and down in it to remove any air trapped by the pour so the concrete will cure properly.

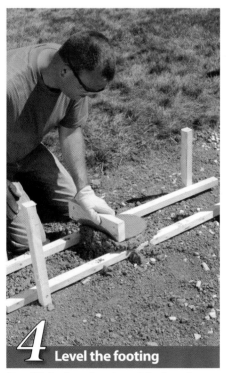

4 Level the footing

Overfill the form by about 2 inches, then screed off (scrape off and level) the excess with a short length of scrap 2×4. Seesaw the screed back and forth to level the mix. Pulling the screed straight across will drag concrete out of the form.

SOAK YOUR PIERS

If you're building a freestanding deck on flat, stable ground where frost heave is not a problem, building codes may allow you to use precast concrete piers instead of footings and posts. If the ground does rise and fall by a small amount, the deck will move as a unit. Because it's not fastened to the house, such movement won't damage the deck or the house.

Some codes require that the piers be bedded in a footing, varying in depth from 1 foot to below the frost line. If your plan calls for bedding precast piers in a footing, be sure to soak the piers in a tub of water for several minutes, then center them in the footing before the concrete sets up. A dry pier will quickly absorb the water from wet concrete, causing it to flake and spall. Such a weakened bond between the pier and concrete could cause the deck structure to fail.

Pouring footings *(continued)*

5 Set the J-bolt

Restring the mason's lines to place the J-bolts. When the concrete begins to set (it will resist finger pressure), push a J-bolt into the center of each form, leaving an adequate thread length exposed. Center each bolt with a plumb bob or tape measure.

6 Square the threads

The exposed threads of the J-bolt must be vertical, or the post anchor will not sit squarely on the footing. Square the threads to the footing with a layout square. Repack loose concrete with a pointed trowel, adding a little more if necessary.

PREPARING A STAIR LANDING

If you want to build stairs that rest on a concrete pad, you can save time and effort by building forms for the pad and pouring it at the same time as your footings. You must determine exactly where the pad will be placed, which is difficult to gauge when the deck hasn't been built yet.

To position the pad, your plans have to be accurate and you have to know where you want the stairs located. See page 91 for information about positioning and building a form for a concrete stair landing.

Installing a wet-insert anchor

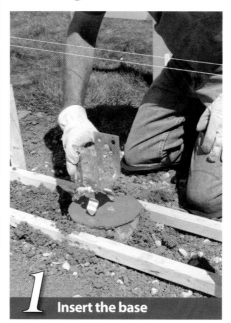

1 Insert the base

Most wet-insert anchors have prongs or a post and must be installed before the concrete sets up. Push the base of the anchor into the center of the footing, rocking it back and forth as you go. Stop when the bottom of the anchor plate touches the footing.

2 Align the anchors

Lay a long, straight 2×4 on the footings, placing it so the edges of all the anchors line up on the same plane. Have someone hold the 2×4 in place while you adjust the position of the anchors.

Drilling an anchor bolt in cured concrete

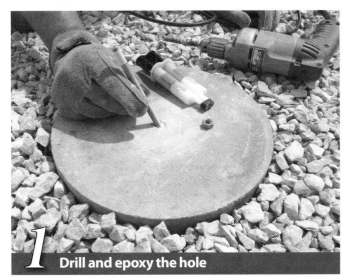

1 Drill and epoxy the hole

Threaded studs that attach post anchors may be installed after the footings have cured. Hammer-drill a hole ⅛ to ³/₁₆ inch larger than the stud diameter and deep enough to leave 1 inch exposed. Wrap the top 1 inch of the stud with masking tape. Blow the dust out of the hole with compressed air. Inject anchor-setting epoxy into the hole and insert the stud immediately.

2 Square the stud

Square the end of the stud to the footing and let the epoxy cure as long as specified by the manufacturer. When the epoxy has cured, measure the height of the stud. If it extends more than 1 inch above the concrete, thread a nut onto the stud and run it down until the top face is 1 inch above the concrete. Cut the stud at the top of the nut with a hacksaw and remove the nut.

Installing posts

■ **TIME:** About 45 minutes to anchor and brace each post
■ **SKILLS:** Measuring, plumbing, driving fasteners
■ **TOOLS:** Hammer, open-end and socket wrenches, drill, tape measure, plumb bob

When you install the posts, you'll employ the same techniques you used laying out the site—measuring, squaring, and aligning. Everything needs to line up precisely. That's where adjustable post anchors have an advantage: They will let you correct most alignment problems.

You can work more quickly if you do everything in stages—set all the anchors loosely and line them up, square all the posts, set and brace them in the anchors, then plumb and align all of them.

1 Set the anchors

Tighten all the anchors in place just enough so you can move the anchor slightly. On the footings parallel to the house, set a long, straight 2×4 across the front edges of the anchors. Line up the anchors so all of them are an equal distance from the house. Tighten each anchor with a socket wrench. Repeat the process on the side posts, setting up the edge of the anchors closest to the house with a plumb bob.

Installing posts *(continued)*

PREP THE POSTS AND RUN THEM WILD

Plumb posts start out square. The day before you set the posts, check each of them and square the ends with a layout square and circular or reciprocating saw. Dip the cut ends in preservative and let the preservative soak in overnight.

You can cut the posts to the specified length before you install them, but slight variations in the footings might cause some to be too short or too long. Instead let the lengths of the posts run wild—with each one taller than you need; you can use a water level to mark them at the same height after installation.

DRESSING ANCHOR THREADS

Setting footings and posts can damage the threads of a J-bolt or stud. Protect the threads with tightly wound tape or by turning a nut onto the threads so that it's even with the top of the bolt.

If the threads of an anchor bolt do become damaged, you can clean them up with a hardened steel die, available at your hardware store. Make sure you get one with the same thread. Turn the die on the threads to recut them and clean out any damage. Absent a die, you can often clean up a damaged bolt with a nut. The nut will suffer some damage in the process, so don't reuse it.

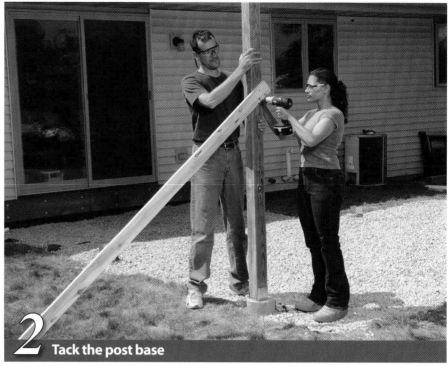

2 Tack the post base

Set each post in its anchor and drive one nail through the anchor hole and about halfway into the post. Have someone help hold the post as plumb as possible. This will keep the bottom of the post in place but will allow you to move it when you plumb it with braces. Tack a 1×4 brace to the post and stake it. Tack and brace the remaining posts. The posts don't have to be perfectly plumb; you can adjust them in later steps.

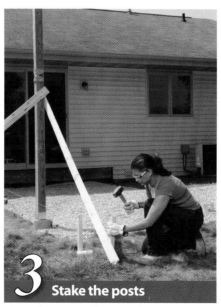

3 Stake the posts

Move the mason's lines on the crosspiece outside the center line by half the width of the post. Restring the lines and clamp a second 1×4 staked brace to the post. Plumb each post with a post level, keeping its outside face against the mason's line.

4 Fasten the posts

Drive the remaining fasteners in the anchors. Some post anchors accept nails or screws only. Others also accept a lag screw. Predrill for the lag screw before driving it.

Marking and cutting posts

■ **TIME:** About 30 minutes per post
■ **SKILLS:** Measuring, plumbing, cutting, driving fasteners
■ **TOOLS:** Framing square, layout square, hammer, post level, tape measure, water level, carpenter's level, reciprocating saw

Posts must be marked and cut accurately. Properly cut posts make the rest of the job go easily and will ensure a sturdy, level deck, so don't rush this step. Ask a friend or two to help so you won't have to move back and forth from one post to another to adjust them.

If time has passed since you set the posts, check them for plumb and readjust them if necessary.

TOP-COAT YOUR POSTS

If you are building your deck with pressure-treated lumber, treat the tops of the posts after you cut them. Although treated wood absorbs preservatives during manufacture, cutting off the end exposes a surface that is less thoroughly treated. To avoid ongoing maintenance problems, brush preservative on the cut ends of the posts. Horizontal surfaces (such as post ends) are most exposed to the weather, but joists and beams need treatment too.

1 Establish the level

Rest one end of a long, straight 2×4 on top of the ledger. Hold the other end against the nearest post. Place a level on top of the 2×4 and level it. Mark the post where the bottom of the 2×4 intersects it. This line is the reference for the next steps.

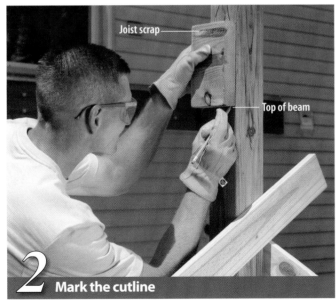

2 Mark the cutline

Joist scrap

Top of beam

Put the top edge of a piece of joist scrap on the reference line and mark the post for the bottom of the joists (top of the beam). Hold the top edge of a piece of beam scrap on this second line and mark the bottom of the beam. This will be the top of the post. You'll cut the posts along this line.

3 Extend the cutline

Hold a layout square on an adjacent post face, level with the cutline. Mark this face and the remaining faces. Cut the post on the line with a reciprocating saw. Set one end of a water level against the cut and the other on the next post. Mark all posts with the water level and cut them.

Installing a beam

- **TIME:** About 3 hours for a doubled 16-foot beam, including assembly and installation
- **SKILLS:** Measuring, cutting, fastening, drilling, caulking
- **TOOLS:** Tape measure, hammer, circular saw, drill, socket wrench, level, post level

A beam runs parallel to the ledger and supports the joists. There are several ways to construct a beam (see photos, right).

A single 4× or 6× beam reduces construction time, but long pieces may be difficult to find. They are expensive and heavy to handle too.

You can build your own beam from doubled lengths of 2× stock. This construction is strong, less expensive, and comes together quickly.

Add ½-inch plywood spacers with pointed tops to a doubled beam to make its width consistent with dimensioned lumber and hardware. The points on the top of the spacers allow water to drain.

Two lengths of 2× stock sandwiched to the sides of posts won't be as strong but may be required because of other factors in your design.

Different deck designs may require you to use a particular method, but local code requirements may determine how you build your beam.

If the beam will rest on top of the posts, strengthen the joint with a post/beam connector.

Use pressure-treated lumber unless you've chosen a naturally rot-resistant wood. Install the beam with its crown side (curved edge) up.

Types of Beams

Single 4× beam

Doubled 2× beam

Doubled 2× beam with spacers

Sandwiched beam

Cantilevering (overhanging) the deck

Joist

Ledger

A = distance from ledger to end of joist

Maximum overhang = A × .333

Beam

Overhang

Cantilevering the front edge of a low deck beyond the beam makes the beam less visible. It will make a ground-level platform seem to float. Joists can usually overhang the beam up to a third of the total joist length. However your local building code may set different requirements; be sure to check cantilever limits. A low deck may be so close to the ground that you won't have room for a large beam. In that case use smaller beam stock and install an additional post.

1 Set the beam

Install post/beam connectors on the posts. Orient the beam openings in the same direction. Position the completed beam assembly in the connectors and center the beam from side to side.

2 Brace the beam

Plumb the face of the beam and brace it on both sides with 2×4s attached to stakes in the ground. A post level will help you keep the beam plumb as you brace it. Brace the beam at other posts.

3 Fasten the beam

Attach the beam to the connectors with screws or nails as specified by the connector manufacturer. Driving screws is less likely to knock the beam out of plumb than driving nails. Remove the braces.

Center joint over post.

Fasten through each spacer from both sides with deck screws.

Building up a beam

4×4 spacers

Machine bolts with washers

Installing a sandwiched beam

A doubled 2× beam with ½- or ⅜-inch spacers will match the width of a 4×4 post. Measure the post width—pressure-treated posts are sometimes a little thinner than other dimension lumber. Point the spacers (pressure-treated plywood) to aid water drainage. Set one board on a solid surface and tack spacers every 24 inches. Set the other member on top and clamp everything together with edges flush. Drive deck screws through each spacer, turn over the beam, then fasten from the other side.

If your deck design requires a 2× sandwiched beam and the face of the beam will be visible, assemble it with ½-inch carriage bolts. If the beam is not visible, use machine bolts with washers on both ends. Support the beam every 24 inches with spacer blocks cut from post stock. Level and clamp both sides of the beam to the posts before drilling the bolt holes; offset the holes to reduce splitting. Tighten the nuts with a socket wrench.

Hanging joists

- **TIME:** 2 hours for a 12×16-foot deck, longer if on a ladder
- **SKILLS:** Measuring, cutting, fastening, squaring
- **TOOLS:** Hammer, tape measure, chalkline, framing square, layout square, circular saw, cordless drill

No matter how many methods of hanging joists you've heard or read about, you should use joist hangers. Most codes require them. Unless you plan to clad the header and rim joists with a fascia, select the straightest and least blemished boards for these pieces—and square the ends before measuring.

Fasten the rim joists and header to the ledger and beam, then hang the inner joists. Building this box structure first is easier than hanging the joists first and attaching the header. If you haven't marked joist locations on the ledger and header, do it after you square the frame.

CROWN SIDE UP

Dimension lumber often has a slightly bowed edge or crown. You can see this crowning by sighting down the edge of the board. Crowning is not a structural problem. The weight of the structure will force it level.

1 Install the rim joists

Measure and cut the rim joists to length—usually 1½ inches shorter than the total front-to-back deck dimension. Rest one end of the first joist on the beam and fasten the other end flush with the ledger using two 3-inch deck screws. Hang the other rim joist in the same way. You can install angle brackets (page 74) at the ledger joint now or after you square the frame.

2 Tack the rim joists

Set a framing square inside the corner at the ledger and again at the intersection of the beam and adjust the rim joists until they are square to the house and the beam. The outer face of the rim joist should be flush with the end of the beam and the end of the joist should be flush with the outer face of the beam (unless you have a cantilevered deck). Tack the rim joists to the beam with a toenail or screw.

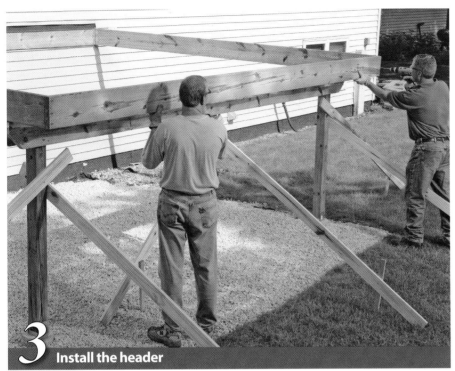

3 Install the header

If you have someone to help, one person should hold the header while the other screws it to the ends of the rim joists. Square the frame with a framing square and check it with a 3-4-5 triangle (see page 31). If necessary remove the toenails at the beam, adjust the joists, and drive the fasteners in again. Set angle brackets in the corners if you haven't already done so. If working alone prop the header, tack one corner, then the other.

(see page 31)

KEEP IT SQUARE

The more care you take to install the joists square with the ledger, the easier the rest of the construction will be. Don't assume you can square things up later. Use a framing square to align each joist at the header. If your joists are all the same thickness, use a spacer to test their spacing. To make the spacer, cut a perfectly square piece of joist stock exactly $14\frac{1}{2}$ inches long. Have a helper use the scrap to space and align the joists at the beam.

4 Mark the hanger locations

Stabilize the frame on the beam with seismic ties (see page 74) and mark joist locations on the ledger and header if you have not done so already. Make sure the joists are spaced as specified on your detailed plans. You can fasten the hangers at the marks as shown here or use the method described in the next step.

(see page 74)

2× flange

5 Install the joists

Cut joists to length and tack a 2× flange at each end of each joist, extending $1\frac{1}{2}$ inches past the ends. The flange keeps the top of the joist flush with the top of the ledger and header. Set the joist on the marks and slide a joist hanger tight to the bottom. Fasten the hanger to the ledger or header. Remove the flanges.

Hanging joists *(continued)*

6 Finish the installation

Continue fastening hangers, nailing or screwing each joist to the hanger as you go. If the header is bowed, have a helper push it toward the joist while you drive the hanger fasteners.

REINFORCE THE FRAME

Seismic tie

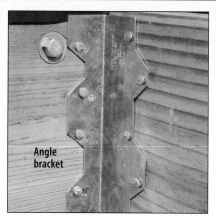

Angle bracket

Framing was once held together by face-nailing or toenailing the joints. Bugle-head (self-sinking) coated deck screws make joints easier to fasten but do not greatly increase the stability of the joint. Framing connectors—such as angle brackets and seismic ties—along with joist hangers greatly increase the strength of framing joints. Most codes require them, but you should use them even if your codes don't specify them.

Blocking the joists

1 Mark the joist centers

Blocking adds lateral stability to a deck frame and provides additional nailing surfaces for some decking patterns. Mark the midpoint of the deck (half the distance from the house to the beam) on both rim joists and snap a chalkline between the marks across the top of the joists.

2 Mark the blocking

Tack a 1×4 on top of each joist near the chalkline to space the joists as your plan specifies. If necessary pull the joists into proper spacing before tacking the board on. Mark the location of the blocking, offsetting the marks as shown.

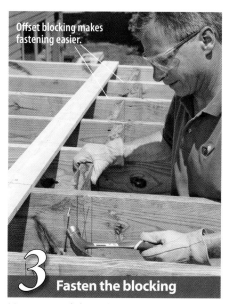

Offset blocking makes fastening easier.

3 Fasten the blocking

Measure each bay (the space between the joists) and cut 2× blocking to fit. Don't cut all the blocks the same size—the thickness of the joists may vary. Install the blocking with nails or screws on alternate sides of your chalkline. Then fasten the joists to the beam with seismic ties.

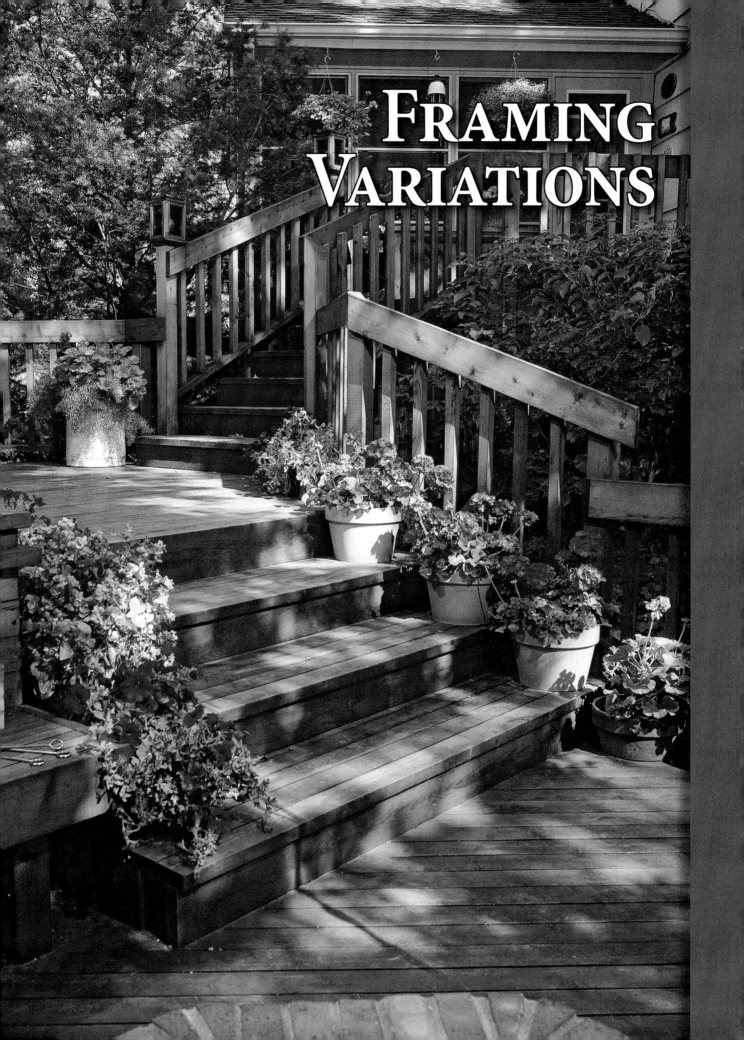

FRAMING
VARIATIONS

Framing a wraparound deck

Plans for a wraparound deck should begin with the decking pattern—the way you want the boards to run. That's because different patterns require different framing—and possibly a different footing layout—to support the deck. The variations shown here, however, are all based on the same footing plan. Decking that runs parallel to the side of the house on each section and meets at a right angle is visually pleasing and the easiest to build (below right).

Decking that turns a corner is attractive but more complicated to frame (top, opposite page). Laying mitered decking can be time-consuming as well, but herringbone corners avoid the need for perfect miter cuts.

Continuous decking (bottom, opposite page) creates a unified appearance. The framing is a bit unconventional, with joists running parallel to the house on one side and perpendicular on the other. The construction, however, is no more complex than for a basic deck.

Lay out the deck

You can approach the footing layout of almost any wraparound deck by thinking of it as two decks with a common post. Set the position of the common post by running a mason's line from the corner of the house to a batterboard. Treat this post as a line post between the two corners. You can square each section with a 3-4-5 triangle or by measuring the diagonals. When the diagonal measurements are equal, the section is square.

Square sections individually by measuring diagonals.

Common post

Perpendicular decking

Framing this wraparound is as easy as framing a single deck—you just do it twice. The foundation for each section starts with its own ledger and ends with its own beam supported by posts and footings. The only peculiarity in this design is the extended ledger. Supporting one section of the deck at the house, it meets with a parallel joist at the corner of the house, and the pair continues to the outside post.

Beyond that, calculate framing requirements, such as post size and spacing and beam and joist spans, as if each section were a separate deck—which it is. This design is an excellent way to enlarge an existing deck with a wraparound section.

Beam

Decking meets at right angle.

Parallel joist

Posts

Extended ledger

Beam

Turning the corner

Decking that turns the corner creates a more interesting pattern and looks more professional than other patterns, but it is more difficult to install. You can turn the corner with butted miters, spaced miters, or herringbone joints.

Butted miters are the most difficult to lay. It's not only hard to cut consistent miters, it's doubly difficult to keep the joints perfectly aligned. Even with perfect cuts, decking boards can be slightly off size, and it only takes a couple of those to throw alignment off in a row of joints.

Spaced miters eliminate this problem. Be sure the doubled joist is wide enough to provide a nailing surface for the mitered ends.

A herringbone pattern is the easiest to install and creates a distinctive look. All of these patterns require miter-cut joists and angled joist hangers.

Butted miters

Common post

Spaced miters

Herringbone pattern

Doubled joist with blocking

Continuous decking

Continuous decking provides an attractive pattern for a wraparound design but requires different framing with two more footings and posts.

Install ledgers on both sides of the house. On the corner that lines up with the common post, add another footing and post and install a beam between the two. Also install an additional footing and post at the corner of the house (top of illustration) and install another beam.

Lap the joists over the common beam and fasten the overlaps together. Plan the decking so the joints don't create an irregular pattern at the corner; usually it is best to start with a piece that runs only partway along the house, as shown at right.

Post

Overlapped joists

Lay this decking board first.

Post

Common post

Common beam

Beam

Posts

Multiple and multilevel decks

Multiple decks work well in a number of settings—both as independent structures and as sections stacked and connected with stairs. Independent multiple decks usually have one deck that acts as a balcony and another that serves as the main deck.

A multilevel design is a good solution for slopes. From a tall main deck, smaller connected decks can stairstep down the slope. These smaller sections won't block the view from the main deck and can work as outdoor rooms in their own right, furnished for small gatherings. Multilevel decks are effective on two-story houses too. You can use the main-floor deck for entertaining, with a lower section off a walk-out basement for a shaded area and a third level off an upstairs bedroom for catching the morning sun. The step-down levels can break up the monotony of a large deck.

Single step down

Lower level needs no railing.

Adjoining levels

Multilevel decks can be built as a series of independent decks linked with stairs. They can also be built with low platforms next to or under each other. In this efficient approach some of the foundation and framing serves both levels. In the example above the upper level is constructed as an individual deck. Posts supporting the beam also support the ledger for the lower level.

When building the framing it often works out well to step levels down by the width of one joist. A 2×8 joist will provide a standard step rise and a 2×6 joist will result in a more gentle step. The lower level can be expanded or offset by shifting post locations. In this example the lower level doesn't require a railing, which adds to the architectural contrast.

Landscaping on many levels

Multilevel decks provide separate areas for different activities and increase landscaping opportunities. Permanent plantings (enclosed in a rough rock wall at the left side of the deck) complement plants in containers on the deck. If the landscape provides only enough room for one full-size deck, use the remaining space to install a platform walk-up. Fill in the other areas with flowers and accents.

Stacked frames change levels

Stacked frames offer an easy way to change levels. Be sure to account for the additional framing weight when computing beam spans and post spacing. Your decking pattern will determine the direction of the joists. If you want parallel decking on both sections, stack the frames with the joists parallel. If you want the decking in one section perpendicular to the other, hang the joists in one section perpendicular to the other. In either case build the lower frame first and hang the joists, then hang the upper frame. Join the levels with metal connectors. A small-scale top frame will function as a step if you need one.

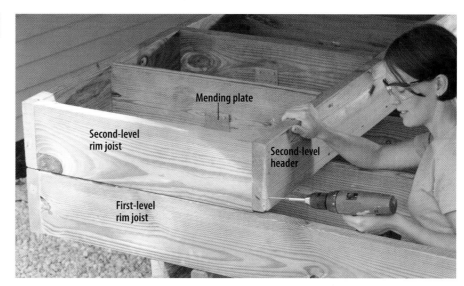

Doubled header

To extend a deck while creating a second level, you might be able to add framing to your existing deck foundation. If the new section is not too large or heavy (use span tables to compute loads, page 44), double the existing header and frame the extension from this point. Add a second-level frame over the first one that extends past the doubled header. This method can be used to frame a succession of gradual level changes.

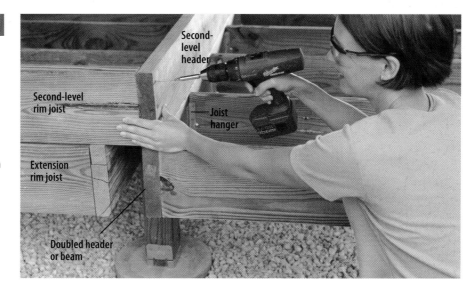

Build individual decks

Sometimes building two or more individual decks is the best solution to raising levels. One level could be attached on one end to a ledger on the house, while the other could be freestanding. Lay out and construct each level with its own footings and framing. Treat each level as a single deck.

It's usually not a good idea to tie these decks together with screws or bolts: If one section settles differently from the other, the stress might crack the frames. If you need a level change more than a 2×6 or 2×8, link them with a step.

Designing elevated decks

People often build houses on steep slopes because of the spectacular views. But the slope may make the yard largely unusable. An elevated deck can solve that problem.

Supported on posts that reach to the main level of the house (or its second story), an elevated deck adds outdoor living space that might otherwise be available only with extensive grading. Flattening or terracing a sloped yard can cause extensive and expensive landscaping problems. An elevated deck might provide an easier solution by bringing the outside surface up to the house.

A deck can have two stories or rise to nearly any height. You can create areas such as a private sunroom or balcony off an upstairs bedroom.

The tall posts, however, create design challenges because the taller they are, the more spindly they look. Use thicker posts than codes require or add trim to smaller posts to make them look more massive. Cover any bracing that codes require with a skirt or plantings.

CAUTION

HIGH ALERT

Building an elevated deck can be difficult, even dangerous. Large posts and beams are heavy, and working with them 10 or 20 feet up can be risky. A tall elevated deck is a job only for a skilled, knowledgeable builder with skilled help and adequate ladders or scaffolding.

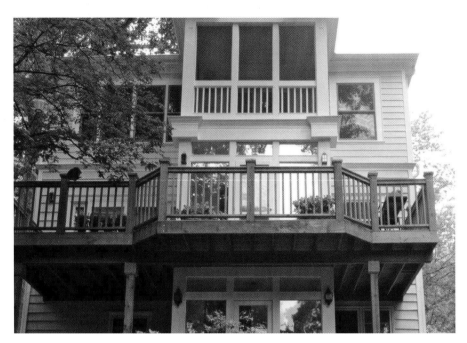

Let the light in

One benefit of an elevated deck is the increased outdoor access from adjacent rooms. Access to the outdoors and increased natural light are highly sought by remodelers. An elevated deck can meet both requirements, but it can also shade lower-level rooms dramatically. If you only need sitting space in your second-story spot, scale the deck back to about 8 feet wide to avoid putting the first-floor rooms in the dark.

Split-level elevation

If you build an elevated deck, consider adding a lower level at the same time, with or without a stairway to the ground. The lower deck shares the same footings and posts, so extra costs are minimal. You could screen the lower level to make a versatile three-season space.

HOW HIGH CAN YOUR DECK GO? (MAXIMUM POST HEIGHT)

Post size	Load area (joist span × beam span)						
	36 sq. ft.	48 sq. ft.	60 sq. ft.	72 sq. ft.	84 sq. ft.	96 sq. ft.	108 sq. ft.
4×4	10'	9'	8'	7'	6'	5'	
4×6	14'	12'	11'	10'	9'	8'	7'
6×6	17'	16'	15'	14'	13'	12'	10'

This table shows maximum post height for Southern pine and Douglas fir (graded No. 2 or better), the most commonly available species of pressure-treated lumber.

To determine the post height for your deck, first compute its load area by multiplying the joist span (the distance between beams or between the beam and the ledger) times the beam span (the distance between posts). The result is the square footage of your load area.

For example, if your deck has joists spanning 8 feet and a beam spanning 6 feet between posts, the load area on the deck equals 48 square feet. Following the appropriate column in the table, you'll see that you can use 4×4 posts up to 9 feet tall. If your deck has a higher elevation, use larger posts. (See page 44 for more on joist and beam spans.)

The post sizing on this table will satisfy most building departments, but verify post sizing with your local inspector. You can use larger posts than are required. On elevated decks 6×6 posts often look better than 4×4s, even if they aren't needed for strength.

More of everything

In addition to taller posts, an elevated deck can require more footings, concrete, and bracing. Other than the size of the materials, construction methods and sequence are the same as for lower decks.

SAFE HEIGHTS

- The maximum acceptable height of posts you can use on a deck depends on several factors, including the size of the post, the species of the wood and its quality, the sizes and spans of joists and beams, and local building codes and regulations.
- Higher decks might require larger posts or closer spacing as well as larger footings.
- If the posts also will support a large overhead structure, check with a design professional or your local building department about the post size to use.

Bracing tall posts

Building codes in many areas—especially where loose soil, earthquakes, or periodic high winds are problems—require post bracing on decks with posts taller than 5 feet. Even if your area doesn't have those problems, bracing can make your deck more stable.

Most bracing can be made with 2×4s, but for braces more than 8 feet long, use 2×6s. Secure braces with ⅜-inch lag screws with washers or carriage bolts with nuts and washers.

Freestanding decks should be braced if they are more than 3 feet above ground. If you don't like the appearance of the exposed braces, add skirting to the posts.

K bracing

Y bracing

W bracing with crosspiece

X bracing

SPACING THE BRACE

4×4 spacer

X bracing or any other style that mounts braces on opposite sides of the posts will create a space where the braces cross each other. Fill the space and increase strength with a spacer the same size as your posts.

The alphabet of braces

Bracing styles are often named after the letters they suggest. The most common types are K and Y and X and W bracing. The strongest bracing ties posts to beams. The style of bracing you employ may depend on appearance and how accessible you want the space beneath the deck to be. But looks may not be everything—building codes may dictate what style to use. To help prevent rot and for neater appearance, miter the joints. When two braces meet on a post, leave a small gap between them to allow for drainage.

Installing decking

- **TIME:** 5 to 8 hours for a 12×16-foot deck, longer for complex patterns
- **SKILLS:** Measuring, cutting, fastening
- **TOOLS:** Tape measure, circular saw, hammer, drill/driver, jigsaw, chalkline, pry bar, layout square, palm sander

Decking is the centerpiece of your deck, so choose it carefully. It gets the most use, takes the most abuse, and is one of the deck's most visible elements.

Building centers generally carry several types and grades of decking material. Pressure-treated (PT) wood is a popular choice, of course, but you can use PT lumber just for the framing and dress up the more visible parts of your deck with fancier stock. See pages 41–43 for more information about selecting lumber.

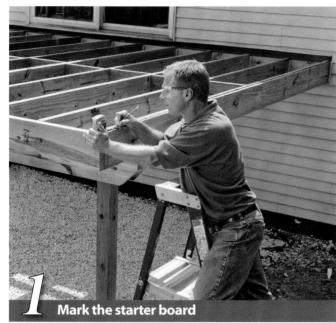

1 Mark the starter board

Measure from the house to the point where the inside edge of the starter board will fall and mark both rim joists at this distance. Snap a chalkline at the marks. Remember that the position of the first board will depend on whether you will overhang the decking or install fascia.

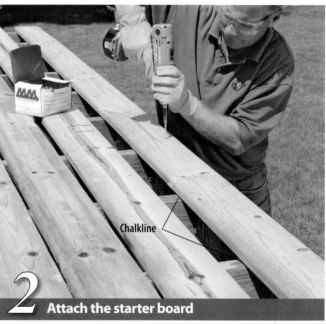

Chalkline

2 Attach the starter board

Lay out the decking boards loosely on the deck. Align the starter board with the chalkline and drive in two screws or nails centered on each joist. If you have joints, offset them randomly and fasten cleats to the sides of the joists for additional support.

TIPS TO BETTER DECKING

Decking is one of the most visible elements of your deck, so install it with care. Naturally resistant woods and KDAT (kiln-dried after treatment) lumber won't shrink much, so they can be installed with uniform ⅛-inch spacing. Make a spacing jig to speed the job (see page 84). PT lumber will shrink after you install it. Fasten PT boards without spacing.

If you install parallel decking, start with the first board at the house or at the outer edge of the deck. Your decking may not come out exactly because of board and spacing widths and the size of your deck, so you may need to rip the last few boards to fit.

If you want to hide the size adjustment, install the full-size starter board at the edge of the deck and finish with the ripped decking next to the house where it will be less noticeable. For diagonal and other decking patterns that begin in the center, you may need to reduce the width of deck boards as you approach the edge.

To make the pattern more attractive, offset the end joints so they do not fall in a straight line. Center the end of the decking on a joist and attach cleats to the joist so you can drive the decking fasteners farther from the end of the board.

PRETREAT THE FRAME AND DECKING

If your lumber and decking were not pretreated, apply water repellent. Start with the joists, posts, and framing—it's much easier to treat them while they're still exposed than to treat them from underneath the deck later.

The day before you install the decking, spray both sides of the decking and let it dry.

3 Space the boards

Set a spacing jig (below) against the starter board and push the next decking board against it. Fasten the second board to the joists, moving the spacing jig along its length as you go. Make sure the decking joints are centered on the joists

and strengthened with 2×4 cleats fastened to both sides of the joist under the joint. Predrill the decking (especially near the ends) to minimize splits. Angle the screws slightly toward the joist to strengthen the connection.

4 Check the spacing

The width of a decking board may vary along its length. One odd board won't make a difference, but several could throw the boards off parallel over the span of a deck. Measure the distance from the house to the board every third row. Adjust the spacing to keep the decking parallel. Snap a chalkline for reference.

MAKE A SPACING JIG

To space decking evenly make a spacing jig from a 1×4 and 10d nails spaced the same as the joist spacing (16 inches, for example). Drive them about an inch through the 1×4. Blunt the tips of the nails so they're less likely to mar or snag on the decking.

STAGGER THE JOINTS

¼" gap

Decking joint

Double joist

Long boards can span a small deck without joints. However a long deck (certainly one more than 20 feet long) will have joints. Plan ahead so you can install double joists in the framing for the joints. When you fasten the

decking, alternately offset the joints as shown above. A small gap between the ends of the boards will improve drainage through the decking and the double joist.

5 Straighten bowed boards

To straighten a bowed board, start one fastener in the board. Drive the blade of a pry bar into the joist and force the decking into place. Hold the board in place with one hand and drive the fastener with the other. Then set the second fastener.

To push a bowed edge away from an adjacent board, start the fastener and insert a pry bar between the boards. Protect the edge you're prying against with a wide putty knife. Force the board into position and hold it. Then drive the fasteners.

WHICH SIDE UP?

Bark side down

Bark side up

Traditional advice is to install decking with the bark side up so water will drain more quickly. It's been debated for about 30 years. Some studies show that decking installed with the bark side down is less likely to develop splits. Other research says it doesn't matter. A practical compromise is to put the best side up and apply a yearly coat of water repellent.

STRAIGHTENING THE STUBBORN ONES

The best way to deal with badly bowed boards is to leave them at the lumberyard. But if one of them has slipped by you, don't throw it away. If a pry bar won't straighten a bowed board, you can probably straighten it with a bar clamp, a long clamp designed to hold together wide glue-ups for tabletops and the like. Set the end hook against a pry bar inserted in a space between the decking. Position the clamp screw against the bowed board. Turn the screw to force the board into place, then fasten it.

Installing decking *(continued)*

6 Adjust spacing in the homestretch

When you get within three boards of the last one, lay them loosely with ⅛-inch spaces. If the last board fits, fasten all three. If not lay two and trim the last one, or rip the excess width evenly from all three.

7 Fasten the last board

Cut the last board to length, including any overhang. You can trim it with a handsaw after it's in place, but cutting it first is easier. Set the board with the proper overhang on both ends, then fasten it.

8 Trim the overhang

Mark the overhang on the face of both the starter board and the last board. Snap a chalkline between the marks. Tack a 2×4 to the deck to guide your saw blade along the line to trim the ends of the decking.

9 Bevel and seal the edges

Produce a professional-looking edge by beveling it with a palm sander, a router with a chamfer bit, or a sanding block and 80-grit paper. Seal the cut edge of the decking before installing the railing.

Notch decking for posts

1 Outline the notch

Set the decking board against the post and mark the edges of the notch on the decking, adding ⅛ inch. Measure and mark the depth of the notch, then lay out the sides with a layout square.

2 Cut and fasten

Cut the notch with a jigsaw and test-fit the cut. Fasten 2× cleats on the post (on both sides of the notch) to provide a nailing surface. Fasten the board to the joist and the cleats.

Installing invisible deck fasteners

- **TIME:** About 8 hours to install clips on a 12×16-foot deck, more for a track system
- **SKILLS:** Measuring, cutting, driving fasteners
- **TOOLS:** Tape measure, layout square, mitersaw, cordless drill, pry bar, hammer

Nail dents, protruding screws or nails, split decking ends, or water puddles in fastener holes will not be problems if you use hidden deck fasteners. Plus the fastener-free surface looks neater.

These fasteners are more expensive than screws or nails, and installation requires substantially more time and labor. Some fasteners, like track rails, are not practical for low decks. The tracks attach to the sides of the joists so you need to be able to fasten deck boards from below.

Joist clips, available in several styles, are the easiest to install. You can work from above, and they hold the boards in place with points that dig into the edges of the boards. They space the boards automatically as you lay them. Recessed clips, made for hardwood like ipe, adapt to any decking. For these you must form recesses in the edges of the boards with a biscuit joiner.

Decking clips

1 Fasten the clips

Fasten the first board as specified by the clip manufacturer. Then attach clips either to the joists or to the edge of the deck boards (shown), depending on the clip style. Use the fasteners that come with the clips; others may not fit.

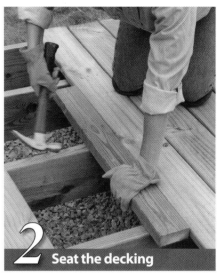

2 Seat the decking

Set the board in place and with a scrap 2×4 on the joist directly behind the clip, seat the board. Start at one end and work your way down gradually. Install the remaining boards the same way.

Track systems

1 Attach the track

Cut sections of track to length, if necessary (some come precut), and line them flush with the top of the joists. Fasten one end, level the track, then fasten the other end. Use only as many fasteners as recommended by the manufacturer.

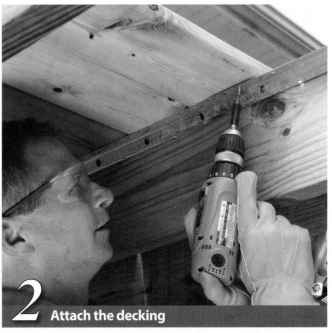

2 Attach the decking

With a helper positioning the decking above, work from beneath the deck to drive fasteners through the track into the decking. Make sure the decking is seated firmly on top of the joists.

Using complex decking patterns

Parallel decking is easy to install and cost-effective. You can enhance its appearance by laying mixed-length boards and staggering the joints. Parallel decking is mostly a practical choice. For a more intriguing look, cover your deck with one of the patterns at right.

The primary concern with any decking pattern is that the framing supports it adequately.

Herringbone, chevron, and basket weave patterns require wider joists for fasteners at the ends of the boards. To install these patterns space joints symmetrically on the deck. At each joint double the joist or triple its width with a 2×4 cleat on both sides. Install full-length pieces first, then place the shorter pieces.

Framing for a modular pattern is similar to standard framing except that some joists are doubled or cleated and blocking is installed between some joists to provide nailing surfaces for the alternating deck boards.

Boards are different lengths with most diagonal patterns. This will create extra work and waste.

Single diagonal

Chevron

Herringbone

With 24-inch joist spacing, the span of deck boards in this pattern is about 34 inches. See Caution box.

Span

Perpendicular

Modular

Basket weave

CAUTION

CHECK DIAGONALS FOR ALLOWABLE SPANS

In a herringbone or other pattern with diagonal boards, the span is the diagonal distance between joists, not the perpendicular distance. The distance may exceed allowable span lengths. If you have doubts about your decking plan, have a professional designer check your plans before you begin construction.

Add a center strip to chevrons

A chevron pattern, or any pattern that requires diagonal cuts to meet at a center point, can be difficult to lay precisely. You can make discrepancies in the cuts less apparent by installing a center decking board as shown above. This pattern requires a double row of blocking to provide a nailing surface for both the center board and the miters. Cut both ends of the boards that go between the house and the strip. On the boards that extend to the edge of the deck, cut the angles and leave the ends wild.

Angle a corner

If the style suits your house, add a 45-degree corner to a deck with overhanging joists. First build the frame square, then measure from the corner an equal amount on the rim joist and header. Cut the joist and header at a $22\frac{1}{2}$-degree angle, then mark and cut the corner piece.

Tips for diagonals

Diagonal decking requires precise 45-degree miters. Practice on scrap before laying your decking. Place a strip of $\frac{1}{4}$-inch plywood against the house as a temporary spacer. On the first two boards, miter one end only and set them on the framing with the miters against the spacer. Measure and mark equal distances from the corner frame to the edges of the boards (this assures the boards are diagonal). Fasten the first, then the second board to the decking with a few screws. Install the remaining boards the same way, then snap chalklines at the joists so you can keep the fasteners in line over the surface of the deck. Trim the wild ends of the boards and remove the spacer.

Attaching a small corner

When you're within 3 feet of a diagonal corner, measure the remaining space to see how wide the last piece will be. Increase the spacing between the last boards so you end up with at least a 5-inch piece. If that doesn't work out, drill pilot holes and fasten the last piece to the adjoining board without spacing.

Building stairs

Almost all building codes have strict standards for stairs. Exterior tread dimensions are often afforded a little latitude, but codes are quite strict about stringers, materials, and overall construction.

Before you start designing your stairway, review stair-building terminology—it can seem confusing at first. Total rise is the vertical distance from the bottom of the stairs to the top of the deck (see page 92). Unit rise is the height of one step. Total run is the horizontal distance the stairway travels.

Unit run is the horizontal depth of one tread from front to back.

After code compliance the most important requirement for outdoor stairs is to make a gradual ascent—short risers and deep treads enhance the safety and comfort of the stairs.

A 3-foot width is the standard minimum, but you may find that a 4- to 6-foot width is more comfortable without adding much to your costs. Use three stringers on stairs 3 feet and wider and add another stringer for every additional 2 feet of width.

- **TIME:** 2 to 3 days to lay out and pour the concrete pad; 5 to 7 hours within that time to lay out, cut, and attach stringers to the deck and treads to the stringers
- **SKILLS:** Working with concrete, measuring, leveling, accurate cutting and fastening
- **TOOLS:** Digging tools, concrete tools, chalkline, drill/driver, hammer, straightedge, tape measure, framing square, level, circular saw, jigsaw or handsaw, sander

Access and design

Stairs serve many purposes in deck designs. They provide access to and from the deck—both to the surrounding landscape and to other levels of the deck. They can greatly increase the seating area of your deck and can be an important element in its style. Stairs come in many forms, from simple, straight-line structures to elaborate multilevel additions with landings. You can install them with or without a landing, but a concrete pad will provide a solid base and a guaranteed long life.

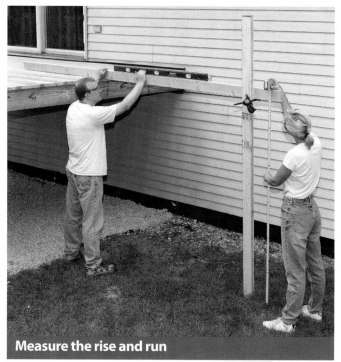

Measure the rise and run

Measure the rise and calculate the run to establish the landing location and the cuts on the stringers. On a level yard measure the rise from the ground to the deck. If the yard slopes (and most do), set a level on top of a long board on the deck and measure down to the ground at the estimated location of the pad. Calculate the run (see page 92) and adjust the pad location to make the steps more comfortable.

Building a landing

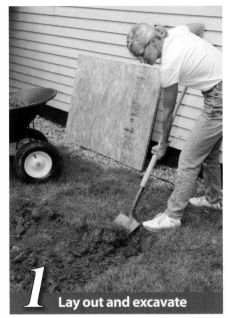

1 Lay out and excavate

A concrete pad 3 to 4 inches thick should rest on 2 inches of gravel and should have reinforcing wire mesh. Lay out the site with a 4×8 sheet of plywood or batterboards and lines (pages 60–61). Excavate 6 inches deep.

2 Build the forms

Use 2×6 lumber to build forms, cutting and staking each piece as you go. Drive the stakes flush or below the tops of the forms so they won't interfere with the screed when you level the concrete (Step 5). Square the corners.

3 Level the forms

Level the forms and make sure their edges are flush at the corners. Shovel in crushed gravel and tamp it. You can tamp this small site with an 8-inch plywood square attached to a 2×4 handle. Tamp the gravel to 2 inches deep.

4 Backfill, reinforce

Backfill the forms to stabilize them. Lay in a section of wire reinforcing mesh. Set the wire on dobies (from your home center) to keep it at the right height or pull it up with a rake when you pour the concrete.

5 Pour concrete, screed

Mix the concrete in a wheelbarrow (page 64) and shovel it into the excavation. Screed the surface (level it) by pulling a long 2×4 across it, seesawing the board. Screed again if necessary and fill low spots.

6 Slip-proof the pad

Smooth the surface with a wood or metal float. Work in wide arcs, keeping the leading edge of the float raised slightly. When the concrete has started to set up (it resists pushing with your thumb), drag a broom across it to make a nonslip surface.

Building stairs *(continued)*

7 Separate the forms

Concrete will stick to wood forms like glue, sometimes even if you coat the forms with motor oil. To get them to pop off more easily, slide a pointed trowel between the concrete and the forms to a depth of about 2 inches.

8 Edge the pad

A round edge on the pad will help prevent chipping. Insert an edger inside the forms and work it back and forth with its leading edge raised slightly. When the concrete has set up, remove the forms and let it cure for a week.

CHOOSE THE RIGHT LUMBER FOR STRINGERS

Stringers carry the weight of the stairs. Choose straight, clear 2×12s with maximum vertical grain. Clear lumber (without knots) is expensive, but it enhances the safety of the stairs.

STEP COMFORTABLY

For safe, comfortable stairs, follow this simple rule: Twice the unit rise (the height of each step to the top of the tread) plus its run (the front-to-back depth of the tread) should equal between 24 and 27 inches.

A standard step has a rise of about 7 inches and a run of 11 inches, for a total of 25 inches.

RISE AND RUN: WHERE WILL IT ALL END?

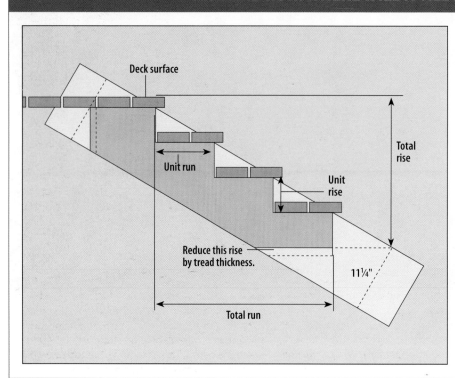

To calculate unit rise divide the total rise (say 30 inches) by the rise you want for each step (7 inches is standard). For this example the result is 4.3.

Round that to the nearest whole number, 4. This is the number of steps necessary to make the total rise.

Divide the total rise by the number of steps to find the actual rise for each step (30 inches÷4=7½ inches). In this case each step is 7½ inches tall.

Multiply the unit run (the depth of the tread cut) you want (11 inches is standard) times the number of steps, minus one (the top step is the deck surface). Here 11 inches×3=33 inches.

Thus the stairway will extend 33 inches from the deck. That's where you should build the landing pad.

Constructing the stairs

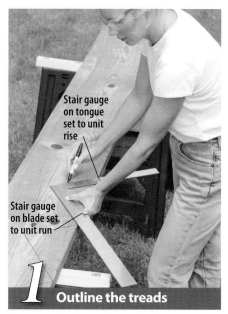

1 Outline the treads

Stair gauge on tongue set to unit rise

Stair gauge on blade set to unit run

Once you've determined the dimensions of the treads and risers, outline the treads on a 2×12. Use a framing square with stair gauges, setting the tongue (the short side) of the square at the unit rise and the blade at the unit run.

2 Cut the stringer

Cut the top and bottom of the stringer and test its fit between the deck and the landing. Then cut the rise and run lines with a circular saw to make an open stringer (see page 95 for closed stringers). Stop each cut just short of the intersection of the lines.

3 Finish the cuts

Finish the cuts with a jigsaw or sharp handsaw but don't cut deeper than the intersection of the lines. Keep the saw lined up in the circular saw kerf.

4 Lay out the remaining stringers

Set the cut stringer on the second 2×12 and position it so you can make the same cuts. Clamp the boards together tightly and use the cut stringer as a template to mark the second one. Hold your pencil at a slight angle to make sure it follows the contour of the cuts exactly.

5 Attach the stringers

Depending on your design you will attach the stringers either to one of the outer joists or to a crossbrace fastened below one of them. Mark the framing for both outside stringers and snap a chalkline between the marks. This line shows the top of open stringers and the plane of metal cleats on closed stringers. Square the stringers to the deck frame and attach them with angle brackets.

Building stairs *(continued)*

6 Add the toe-kick

There are several ways to anchor the bottom of the stringers ("Attachment Options"). These stringers have been notched for a toe-kick—a 2×4 fastened to the concrete pad. Cut the toe-kick and predrill holes for lag screws, then position the toe-kick. Using the predrilled holes

mark the pad with a small masonry bit. Remove the toe-kick and drill the pad with a masonry bit to fit the lag-screw shields. Attach the toe-kick to the landing with lag screws and attach the stringers to the toe-kick with nails or deck screws.

ATTACHMENT OPTIONS

Gravel base

2×4 (anchor with landscape spike)

Angle bracket

Lag shield

Lag screw

Concrete base

Attach stringers to landing. On a gravel pad attach two 36-inch 2×4s to the bottoms of the stringers and drive landscape spikes through them into the gravel. On a concrete pad space the outside stringers 36 inches apart, center the middle stringer, and attach with lag screws and shields.

7 Fasten the treads

If your outside stringers are open, cut the treads with a 1½-inch overhang on both sides. If the stringers are closed (page 95), cut the treads to fit between them. Predrill holes for the fasteners—three per joint for a 2×12 or 2×10 tread, two for narrower boards. Fasten the treads to the outside stringers with nails or screws, then from underneath, fasten the tread to the stair brackets.

8 Add a professional edge

Once the treads are in place, chamfer the edges to improve their appearance. You can use a palm sander or a sanding block and 80-grit paper. A block plane would also work. Whatever the method, keep the angle as consistent as possible.

Making closed stringers

1 Outline the treads

Steps attach between closed stringers. Using a framing square outline the tread locations on the stringer stock (see page 93). Outline the thickness of the tread and mark the location of the cleat as shown above. This makes it easier to position the stair cleats (see Step 2). Make the top and bottom cuts and test-fit the stringer between the deck and ground.

2 Attach stair cleats

You can fasten stair cleats to the closed stringers either before or after attaching the stringers to the deck. If you're doing it before, set the 2×12 on a work surface with the cleats and fasteners within reach. Position one end of the cleat on the line and predrill one fastener hole. Drive the fastener at this end, line up the cleat, and predrill and drive the remaining fasteners. Install the remaining cleats.

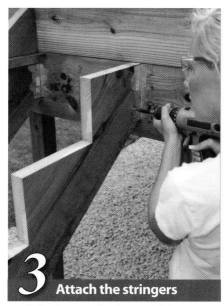

3 Attach the stringers

Mark the framing for the top of the stringers and snap a chalkline. Attach the stringers to the framing with angle brackets, then square them. Fasten the stringers to the landing. If the stairs are wide closed stringers may be combined with one or more open stringers for support in the middle.

A solid stringer alternative

You can fasten the treads to closed stringers with either wooden cleats or metal stair brackets. Steps fasten to the brackets from underneath, which can make them more difficult to install but leaves the fasteners invisible. Don't rely on screws or nails driven from the outside of the stringer into the ends of the treads. You can apply construction adhesive between wooden cleats and the stringers and steps.

4 Attach the treads

Fasten the treads to the cleats with the fastener of your choice (or the one required by local codes). Depending on the height of the stairs and the amount of room underneath, this can be difficult.

Always work from the top down to make it easier to reach under the treads. Fasten the ends of the treads first, then the middle brackets.

NOTCHING A POST

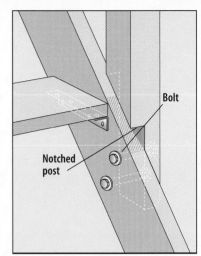

If posts support both the stringer and a stair railing, consider notching the posts to improve the looks of your stairs. Set the post in place, plumb it, then mark the intersection of the stringer and post. Cut the notch and fasten with bolts.

CAUTION

FOR COMFORT AND SAFETY ADD HANDRAILS

Municipal codes generally require a railing on stairs with three or more risers. But all stairs are safer if you add a railing. Everyone understands the added security of having a solid object to grasp when moving from one step to the next. Railings are important if your deck is going to be used by the very young or old. Think safety even if your deck has a one-step level change. Avoid stumbles by adding a strip of yellow reflective tape to steps for greater visibility.

Add a stair railing

Match the stair railing with the deck railing style. Use similar balusters spaced at the same interval.

Handrails must be easy to grasp. A 2× cap rail will make the stairway safer.

Prepare and fasten posts and balusters the same way as for the deck railing (pages 97–100). Make plumb cuts on the top rail.

Installing railings

- **TIME:** About 16 hours to build railings for a 12×16-foot deck
- **SKILLS:** Measuring, cutting, fastening, leveling
- **TOOLS:** Circular saw, mitersaw, post level, 4-foot level, 2-foot level, layout square, drill/driver, spade bits, twist drill, socket wrench, jigsaw, hammer, water level, chisel, clamps, tape measure

Railings are more than a safety feature for your deck. They also help establish the deck's style and set the limits of its space. Local building codes define standards for a safe deck railing (see the drawing at right). Within those standards you can apply an almost endless number of design choices and construction techniques.

The most common railings are similar to a traditional picket fence. A typical framework consists of 4×4 posts bolted to the outer joists, spanned by 2×4 rails and a 2×6 cap rail, with the balusters providing the infill and much of the style.

The photos on pages 97–100 show a simple, attractive design. Like most railings the rails are attached first, then balusters, then the cap rail.

When installing the posts the deck overhang will get in the way, but you can either notch the post or notch the decking so the bottom of the post rests flat against the joist. Notching the decking reduces the possibility of weakening the posts.

To prevent sagging railings keep the spans between posts at 5 feet or less and use rails-on-edge designs. Bolt each post to the frame with two $7/16$-inch bolts. Creating level lines is especially important because railings are seen against the background of the house. Use a water level—not a line level or level-and-long-board—for maximum accuracy in building railings.

Maximum spacing specified by code = 4"

2×2 = 1½"

Distance between posts = 60"

Calculate baluster spacing

Building codes specify the maximum baluster spacing. Here's how to calculate uniform baluster spacing.

Add the width of one baluster (here $1\frac{1}{2}$ inches) and the maximum spacing (4 inches). Divide this total ($5\frac{1}{2}$ inches) into the space between posts to find the number of balusters: 60 inches÷$5\frac{1}{2}$ inches =10.9. Round up to 11 balusters.

Then calculate the actual spacing. Multiply the number of balusters by the width: $11 \times 1\frac{1}{2}$ inches=$16\frac{1}{2}$ inches. Subtract that from the post spacing: 60 inches−$16\frac{1}{2}$ inches=$43\frac{1}{2}$ inches. Divide this by the number of spaces, which is always one more than the number of balusters, to determine the final spacing between balusters: $43\frac{1}{2}$ inches÷12=3.625 or $3\frac{5}{8}$ inches.

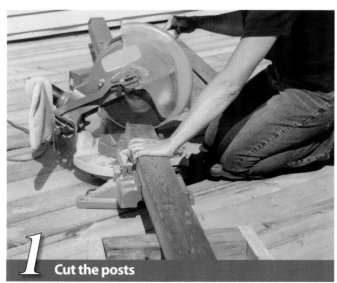

1 Cut the posts

Cut your posts to a height equal to the height of the railing plus the thickness of the decking and width of the outer joists—minus the thickness of the cap rail. Build a jig so you can cut all posts to the same length. Angle the bottom of the posts as an accent.

2 Mark the bolt holes

Mark the location of the bolt holes—about 1 inch from the sides of the post and 1½ inches from the top and bottom of the joist. Stagger the holes to reduce splits. A template will keep the holes consistent. Drill holes the same diameter as the bolts.

Installing railings *(continued)*

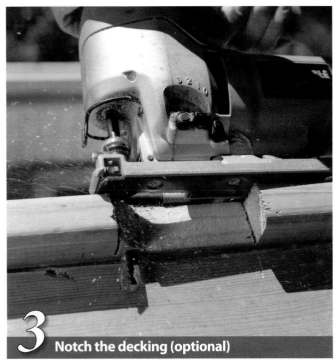

3 Notch the decking (optional)

Measure each post before you mark the notch on the decking—the width of pressure-treated stock is often inconsistent. Mark the sides of the notch 1/8 inch wider than the post so you don't have to force it to fit. Use a jigsaw to notch the decking. Number each notch and its corresponding post on masking tape.

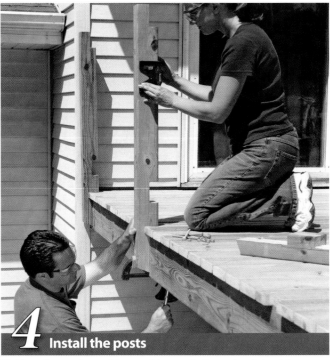

4 Install the posts

Hold each post in position and have a helper plumb it with a post level. Whether working alone or with a helper, clamp the post to the joist. Using the holes in the post as a guide, drill holes of the same size through the joist. Insert carriage bolts through the holes and tighten washered nuts with a socket wrench.

ANCHORING THE END OF THE RAILING

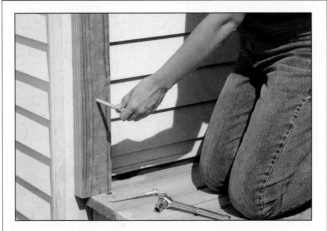

Instead of fastening a post where the deck meets the house, use a 2×4 end rail. Cut the 2×4 to the height of the railing and fasten it to the siding with 5-inch lag screws and washers. This connection is far sturdier than a post fastened to the joists and will add stability to the entire length of the railing.

PRODUCTION NOTCHING

To notch several posts, gang them (clamp them together with their faces flush) and use a layout square or combination square to outline the dimensions of the notch. Cut what you can with a circular saw (use a guide if possible) then chisel out the rest (see page 100). Use the same techniques for gang-cutting other railing members.

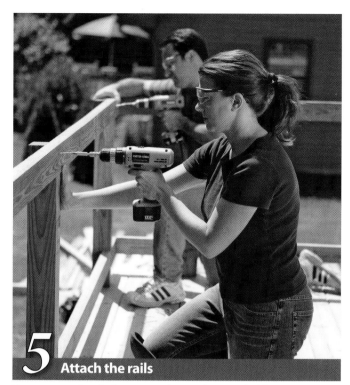

5 Attach the rails

You can attach rails flat or on edge, with toenailed fasteners, wooden cleats, or metal brackets. Whatever method you use predrill the holes to prevent splitting.

6 Cut the balusters

Cut the balusters to the same length with a stop block or cutting jig. Assemble the jig so it supports the end of the baluster and puts the cut end along the fence of your mitersaw. Or clamp the balusters together and cut several of them at the same time.

7 Install the balusters

Build a jig like the one shown to plumb balusters and space them uniformly. Check every fourth or fifth baluster with a 2-foot level to make sure it's plumb. Baluster stock is not always a consistent width; you may have to adjust the spacing slightly to make everything come out right.

JOINTS IN THE TOP RAIL

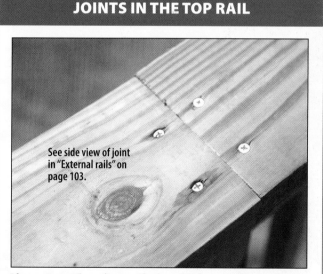

See side view of joint in "External rails" on page 103.

If your top rail won't span the length of your railing, join shorter sections with a scarf joint, two 45-degree bevels that meet straight. Measure from the corner to the center of a post and cut a scarf joint there with a mitersaw. Drive two fasteners on each side of the joint.

Installing railings *(continued)*

8 Fasten the cap rail

Cap rails are usually cut from 2×6 stock. Cut the rail to length and miter-cut one end. If the board is not long enough to span a railing section, cut a scarf joint in the other end so it will be centered on a post. Fit the cap rail on top of the railing with an even overhang on each side. Attach with two 2½-inch screws in each post and one in the top rail every 2 feet between posts.

9 Snug the corners

Miter joints add style to the corners of a deck, but they are difficult to cut straight and they often separate after about a year. Cut the miter as shown below and drive #8 screws to draw the sides of the joint together. Then drive fasteners into the posts.

NOTCHING A POST

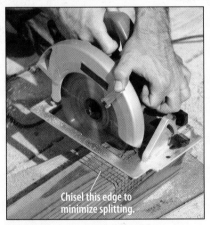

Chisel this edge to minimize splitting.

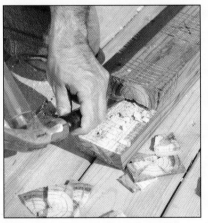

Whether gang-cutting a number of posts or notching a single post, cut kerfs in the notched side with a circular saw. The closer the cuts the more precise your notch will be.

Remove the waste wood from the notch with a hammer and clean out the face of the notch with a sharp 1-inch wood chisel. Do not sand the surface; sanding will result in rolled edges.

CUTTING PERFECT MITERS

Make your miters match. A miter will have a gap if the corner is not square. You can't square the corner, but you can modify the miter. Cut both sides of the joint and tack or clamp the cap rail in place. Cut through the joint with a circular saw, remove the rail pieces, and attach them tightly.

Customize your railings

Railings offer countless ways to personalize your deck. Baluster styles, post spacing, materials, and ornaments can make striking changes in the appearance of your railing—and your deck. Even the method used to mount the rails will affect the style of your deck. Mount bottom rails flat or on edge inside the post bays or on edge on the surface of the posts. Mount long rails on edge in notched posts. Mount top rails inside the bays or continuously on top of the posts. Insert 2×2 balusters, slats and battens, acrylic sheet, or lattice panels. Even the most common beveled baluster design will look different from others with a 2×6 cap rail, finials, and post caps. Make sure your design meets local code requirements for railing height and baluster spacing.

Post options

Full post

Full posts provide solid support. They fit into notched decking and are easier to install than other designs.

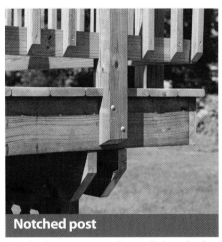

Notched post

Notched posts give railings a lighter look but provide slightly less lateral strength than full posts. Increase the strength of the railing with rails set on edge.

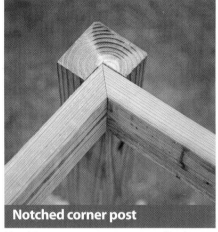

Notched corner post

Notching a corner post saves on lumber costs over a double-post corner (see page 102). It imparts a smooth look that fits well into a contemporary theme.

Cutting corner notches

Crosscut mark

Cut the notch

Outline the notch with a carpenter's pencil so you can see the line when the sawdust flies. For a side post set the saw to the maximum depth and cut the long lines on each side. Don't cut past the crosscut mark. For a corner post set the blade depth to 1½ inches and make the long cuts. Finish the crosscut with a handsaw.

Finish a corner post

Make both the long cuts and a shallow crosscut. Chisel toward the crosscut with a sharp 1-inch wood chisel to clean out the waste. Continue along the length of the notch in repeated passes until all the waste is removed and the faces of the notch are clean.

STRENGTHEN A NOTCHED POST

Install additional framing to support notched posts. On a header add 2× blocking between the joists. On rim joists add blocking between the interior joists to reduce flexing.

Customize your railings *(continued)*

Single-post corner set inside joists

Post

45° mitered corner

Cap rail

Outer joist

Double-post corner with notched posts

45° mitered corner

Posts

Cap rail

Outer joist

Mitered framing

22½° mitered corners

Posts

Cap rail

Outer joist

Turning corners

You have a choice of designs for the corners of your railings. Setting posts inside corners (hanging the joists on the outside faces of the posts) provides excellent through-post support for overhead structures. You can use this method to support railings on the corners of a cantilevered design.

A two-post corner is the most common design and offers the most lateral strength because side loads, such as people leaning

on the railing, are carried by both posts. This construction looks especially good when the spaces between the posts are filled with balusters.

Mitered framing lends distinction to a cantilevered design and enhances a common rectangle.

Installing through posts

Railing height

Notch decking here.

Interior joist

Machine bolt

Header

Blocking

Interior joist

Rim joist

Through posts

Through posts rest on footings and continue upward to support railings or overhead structures. They are most often installed inside the outer joists so you'll have to notch the decking around them.

This design will put the remaining posts inside the framing. If your post spacing allows it, attach these line posts where an interior joist meets the header. The line posts do not go to the ground.

If a line post falls in the middle of a rim joist, add perpendicular blocking and fasten it from both sides to keep the post from tilting under stress.

Rail options

Predrill toenailed fasteners at 45°.

Rail

Cut scarf joints in surface-mounted rails and predrill.

External rails

Mark the height of the bottom rails on the posts and attach them to the posts with two fasteners, three at the corners. Attach the top rail flush with the top of the posts.

Notched posts

Cut the notches 1½ inches deep and select rail stock with uniform thickness. Fasten the rails with two fasteners, centering joints on the posts.

Making modular infill

5/4 decking supports and centers 2×2 balusters on 2×4 rails.

1 Assemble the parts

If the spacing between your posts is uniform (in most cases it should be) and your design includes internal infill units, you can save a lot of time by assembling all the units at once, then installing them inside the posts.

Set up your construction zone on a clear area of the deck. Tack two decking boards to the deck to support both ends of the balusters and mark the baluster spacing on both of them. This will keep the balusters centered on the rails. Lay the precut railings edge down and drive one fastener through the rail into each baluster. Attach the remaining rail. Build the rest of the units and fasten them to the posts.

2 Clamp the units

Railing units can be installed a lot faster and more exactly if you clamp them in place before driving the fasteners. Support both ends of the bottom rail on scrap to keep the rail level and in place. Clamp the first baluster to the post and drive screws through predrilled, angled holes.

Customize your railings *(continued)*

Rail, baluster, and post styles

As long as you meet code specifications for spacing and height, what you use to fill in the space between posts is largely up to you. (Some local codes may not allow glass panels or horizontal infill.)

Rails that are installed on edge on either the inside or outside post faces are least likely to sag. Flat rails tend to sag, but you can reduce or even eliminate sagging by centering a 4× support post between the rail and the decking. Fasten flat rails to the posts with rail brackets, toenailed fasteners, or wooden cleats, or set them into dadoes cut in the posts.

Railing materials also offer a variety of design options. You can use copper or galvanized steel tubing instead of wood balusters. Copper can be lacquered or coated with a plastic or polymer finish to preserve its color or you can let it age to a blue-green. Steel or aluminum balusters can be inserted as is or painted.

Clear acrylic sheets or glass, where allowed, maintain an open view. Welded wire mesh hog fencing could be used to make strong and attractive infill.

Local codes may prohibit horizontal infill because children can use it as a ladder to climb over the railing. But if kids and codes are not issues in your design, make plain but stylish infill from horizontal 1×4s or 2×4s. Metal tubing or thick wood dowels offer an attractive alternative.

Whatever you use remember that wear and gravity will make most horizontal elements sag. Make sure they are strong and solidly supported.

Lattice railing infill provides more privacy than standard railings, yet allows plenty of air to circulate. The lattice can be fixed in place with stops nailed to the posts and to top and bottom flat rails (see page 120).

Edge rails, balusters on joists

Edge rails, balusters on rails

Flat rails, set on posts

Flat rails, set between posts

Flat rails, set into dado

Steel or copper tubing

Lattice

DECK VARIATIONS

Designing an entryway deck

Decks are normally thought of as backyard structures for fun and sun. But they are also appropriate for front entries, although they may require design refinements.

An entryway deck probably will be visible from the street, so you should hide the foundation and framing with lattice, solid skirting, or well-designed planting beds. While it's important to integrate a backyard deck into the overall design of your home, it's doubly important for a deck on the front of your home.

With a well-designed portico roof or other overhead structure, an entryway deck looks like an old-fashioned front porch. For entry stairs consider adding risers to close the back of the steps. Design your railing with special care.

A careful update
Extending the entry, adding a side porch, and incorporating stylistic elements (including the solid skirt) appropriate to the house has updated this 1920s entry without conflicting with the house's Tudor lines.

Staging your entrance
This graceful, gradually staged entryway deck is made from a series of platforms that ease the ascent to the doorway. The middle platform features a roomy built-in bench. Metal railings, common on entryways, help reinforce the deck's front entryway function. Landscaping plays a role too; hidden lights illuminate the pathway at night, and tall bushes hide the structure of the platforms.

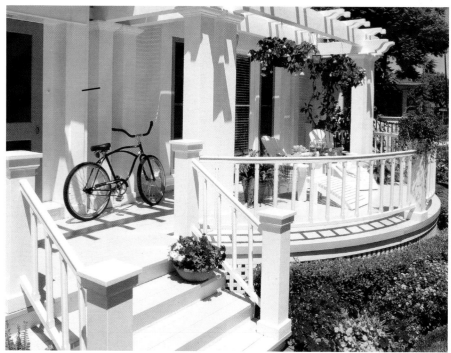

Fitting style
A front-door deck may require more renovation so the new complements the old. The appropriate style of overhead structure with distinctive rafters and arches can do just that. This pergola is not made for shade. Its real function is to enhance the entry without interfering with the sunlight.

Building freestanding decks

A freestanding deck is a self-supporting structure. It can go just about anywhere—out in the yard or right next to the house but not connected to it.

Why build a freestanding deck next to the house? If you want to construct two or more cascading platforms, it would save you the trouble of attaching ledgers to the house on multiple levels. Also the style or construction of the house might not allow you to install the necessary ledgers.

A freestanding deck in a remote part of the yard can take advantage of a great view or a particularly private spot. Overlapping freestanding platforms can create a gradual stairway to a main deck.

A modular deck (pages 108–110) is the simplest of freestanding decks and needs no foundation. In fact freestanding decks often do not need footings at all. They are often built on precast piers—perhaps with shallow footings. A freestanding deck with piers won't be damaged by frost heave—all the piers or footings will rise and fall at the same time.

Keep framing about 1½" away from siding.

Posts in concrete footings (optional construction)

Create an independent foundation

A freestanding deck is built in the same way as an attached deck, except that two (on long decks, more) footings and posts and an additional beam replace the ledger. These elements might increase construction cost, time, and labor. Consider those factors when weighing design options for your deck.

REASONS FOR A FREESTANDING DECK

Where soil is unstable, deck builders often build freestanding decks to avoid problems caused by uneven settling. Many professional deck builders design all their decks as freestanding units because a ledger traps moisture against the siding, which can rot the deck and the house framing. Digging and pouring a few more footings, however, is usually more work than installing a ledger.

1 Lay out and frame

Prepare the site, lay it out, then locate and dig footings. Install posts. Build the frame and square it by measuring the diagonals. If piers are your only foundation, bed the piers and assemble the frame in the piers. Square the frame.

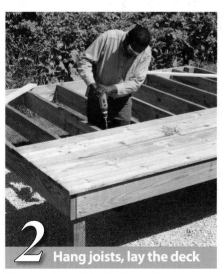

2 Hang joists, lay the deck

Once you're certain the frame is square, tack 1×4 braces across two corners. Start installing the decking at the other end, keeping the boards spaced at ⅛ inch. When you reach the braces, remove them and finish the decking.

Creating modular decking

■ **TIME:** 1 hour to build the jig and about 1 hour for each module

■ **SKILLS:** Measuring, cutting, fastening

■ **TOOLS:** Basic carpentry tools

These basic panels, often called duckboards, are easy to build and can be combined into many shapes for an attractive parquet design. If you have a level yard and soil that does not get soggy, modular units can last a long time. If you lay them on a firmly tamped bed of gravel, they will remain fairly stable.

If you are going to use modules in high-traffic areas or find that they have more spring to the step than you'd prefer, reinforce the center of each module with an extra 2×4 cleat.

COVER AN OLD PATIO

An old concrete patio that's stained and cracked is an ideal candidate for a modular makeover. First make sure the distance from the patio surface to the threshold of the patio door is enough to accommodate the modules. If it isn't quite enough, modules with flat 2×4 or 2×2 cleats might fit. Measure the patio and size the modules to fit the surface.

As you install the modules, shim them with cedar shim shingles as necessary to create a flat surface. You can attach the modules to the concrete surface with construction adhesive for more stability.

MIX THINGS UP

Combine decking modules with pavers, brick, flagstone, or other materials to create a landscape feature. A module or a group of them in the middle of a garden would provide a place for a table and chair. A single module could be built as a hexagon or octagon for added interest.

Use modules to form any pattern

Modular construction is, by its nature, versatile and adaptable. You can use a modular approach to build a basic ground-level deck like the one above.

You could lay out a larger deck or arrange modules as several decks joined by walkways. Modules could be laid around raised garden beds to create a boardwalk.

Mix and match modules

You can probably think of several projects that could combine modular construction with standard deck-building techniques. Here modules make a boardwalk from the house to a side deck—a great way to avoid the costs and labor of building a separate platform. If your needs or tastes change over the years or if you simply want a change, just pick up the modules and rearrange them. You can stack them to make low steps. Alternate the direction of the decking for a parquet effect, as shown, or lay them in the same direction for continuous lines.

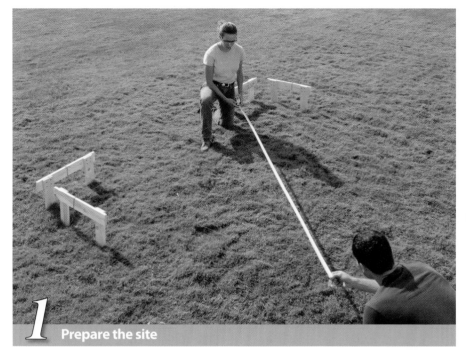

1 Prepare the site

Use batterboards and mason's lines to outline the perimeter of the site, including a 3-inch sand border. Square the corner by measuring a 3–4–5 triangle (page 31) and stake the corners with a plumb bob. Run lines between the corner stakes and mark the outline on the ground (pages 60–61). Remove the sod and soil to 5 inches deep. Spread 3 inches of gravel on the site and level and tamp it. Add 2 inches of sand, level, and tamp.

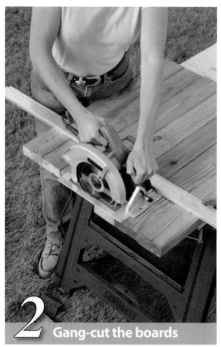

2 Gang-cut the boards

Each module calls for 10 pressure-treated 2×4s, each 29 inches long. Cut them quickly by clamping several 2×4s edge-to-edge, then cutting them in one pass with a circular saw. Use a straightedge to guide the saw.

3 Build a jig

To produce identical modules make this jig from pressure-treated 2×4s about 3 feet long. Make sure that the inside edges are straight, then fasten the boards at the corners to leave a 29×29-inch inside framing area. Align the corners with a framing square as you fasten the boards together. The jig doesn't have crossbracing, so check it for square after assembling each module.

SAVE THE SOD

Reuse the sod and topsoil you remove from your deck site. Before you excavate the site, take a look at areas in your yard that could use some sod patching. To make sod easier to reuse, cut it into strips with a spade, then work the spade under the sod and dislodge the roots. Roll the sod and water it after transplanting it. If you do throw the sod on the compost pile, put the grass side down to stop it from growing. Add the topsoil to garden beds.

Creating modular decking *(continued)*

2×2 guide

Module cleat

Jig

Temporary brace

4 Build the modules

Set the jig on a solid, flat surface, then tack a 2×2 guide on one side to keep the ends lined up. Each module requires eight 2×4 deck boards and two 2×4 cleats. Set the cleats on edge at the sides of the jig.

Attach the decking with 2½-inch decking screws. Space the boards ⅛ inch apart. The width of 2×4s varies, so you may need to adjust the spacing to make the last piece even with the cleat.

5 Set the modules

Lay the modules on the sand bed, alternating the direction of the boards. Attach modules to each other by drilling pilot holes and toenailing, as shown.

WOOD PATH

Building and installing deck modules is easier than pouring a concrete walkway or laying a brick sidewalk. A boardwalk can connect the house to the garage or the house to a modular deck. Enlarge the jig shown on page 109 to build a 36-inch (or wider) path. Larger modules will require additional cleats in the center. By excavating you can set the modules level with the grade.

6 Trim the edges

Once you have assembled the modules in a pattern, you may want to trim the edges for a more finished look. Cut two 1×4s to fit flush on opposite ends and two others for the edges.

You may have to remove some sand so you can fasten the trim flush with the decking. Replace the sand and tamp around the edges.

Spa surrounds

Wood and water make perfect companions, perhaps because of their mutual natural origins. A deck surface surrounding a pool does more than enhance the looks of the whole. It's a surface that will withstand years of use—making a spa, hot tub, or swimming pool a natural long-term partner for a deck.

To get to that point, you'll need to make special preparations. The water in a spa, hot tub, or pool will weigh a ton or more, and local building codes will probably require a ground-level reinforced concrete pad (see page 112).

The spa, hot tub, or pool will require an opening in the deck, so you'll need special framing (see page 112).

The amount of space required depends on the size of the hot tub or spa. Small spas can fit easily within a 12×12-foot surface. Privacy and shade are important, so put the deck out of sight or plan effective screening.

Pools and hot tubs require plumbing and electrical connections too. Hide these systems behind framing or skirting. Build pullout or hinged hatches into the decking or make skirting sections removable for repairs and maintenance.

Code requirements for fencing around pools and spas are strict—access to the location usually has to be childproof. With careful planning you may be able to provide the required safety fencing with a railing system on the deck.

Raise the spa

A spa or hot tub can provide a striking deck accent when the rim sits above the deck surface. The raised pool reduces the danger of falling into the water accidentally. A tub or spa must sit on a concrete pad or adequate framing set on posts and footings; standard deck framing will not support the weight. Add built-in seating around the spa and an overhead structure for shade. Consult local building code officials before you plan for a spa or hot tub on your deck.

Drop in a tub

Setting a spa or hot tub flush with the deck surface makes it easy for you to sit on the edge with your feet in the water. The rim of the unit will not support the weight of the spa; support must come from additional framing or a concrete pad underneath. Safety is a primary concern because children and adults can easily fall in. A sturdy cover and adequate supervision are essential.

Spa surrounds *(continued)*

Building an elevated pad

Build an elevated pad following the same techniques as for a ground-level pad—laying out the site with batterboards, building and staking forms, and pouring the concrete (page 91). But for this foundation you should order concrete delivery from a ready-mix truck. An elevated pad for a spa or hot tub can easily require 15 cubic feet or more of concrete—a volume that's impractical to mix by hand.

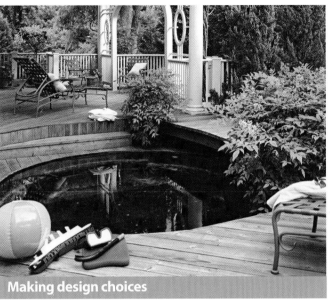

Making design choices

Commercial suppliers offer a broad selection of spas and hot tubs that can be installed on (or in) a deck. To choose one, first decide the general theme of your deck design, then determine the general location of the spa. Find one that fits—both structurally and visually—then round out your design and your detailed plans with the spa as the focal point.

CAUTION

SAFETY UNDERFOOT

Most people will be barefoot on the deck surrounding a pool or hot tub. Be sure you make the surface safe. Buy the best grade of decking you can afford. Radius-edge decking in a naturally resistant species is a good choice. Redwood does not splinter as easily as cedar or pressure-treated wood, so its higher cost may be worth it for a tub surround. Take care of popped-up screws or nails as soon as they appear. Reseal the wood at least twice a year and sweep the deck regularly—twigs and stones can hurt feet too.

Concrete pad supports tub.

Framing a tub surround

A recessed water feature can never have any part of its weight borne by its rim. You have to center the opening in the framing exactly above the supporting pad. Begin by building the pad a little larger than the minimum dimensions specified by the manufacturer. That will allow you to adjust the framing slightly from one side to the other in case actual measurements don't quite match your detailed plans. Block the framing so it supports all the edges of the decking.

DECK FEATURES

Building planters

■ **TIME:** 1 or 2 hours, depending on the planter
■ **SKILLS:** Cutting, fastening
■ **TOOLS:** Circular saw, hammer, cordless drill, layout square, framing square

Planters overflowing with annuals and perennials can soften the lines of your deck and help link it to your landscape.

Whatever planter you make be sure that water can drain freely out of the bottom and plan where that water will go. Drained water trapped in a cavity below the planter can cause decking to rot. Most decorative plants need less than 1 foot of soil depth. Rather than filling a tall planter with more soil than necessary, build a shelf inside it.

Make the planter 18 to 24 inches deep if you will plant shrubs or bushes. Planters for annuals can be smaller. Always build planters with an inch or two of space beneath them to allow for air circulation.

Mitered corner · Waterproof liner · 2×2 · Ripped 5/4×6 cap rail · Pressure-treated plywood · 1×2 cleat · Drainage holes · 5/4×6 decking

RECYCLE DECK SCRAPS

When you've paid for good-quality lumber, the last thing you should do is add it to the landfill or burn it in the fireplace. Instead save scraps to build small outdoor projects. (Never burn pressure-treated wood; it releases toxins into the air.)

You'll likely have enough scrap to build a planter or two. Set the planters in corners, along the edge of the deck, or on top of railings. Pressure-treated wood is fine for planters, but redwood and cedar make more attractive boxes.

Basic planter construction

All planters are basically boxes—four sides and a bottom, perhaps with some kind of optional legs and a cap rail for appearance. Almost any lumber will do; using decking boards for the sides adds to the unity of the deck design. Although you can fasten the corners without corner blocks, using them will create a stronger container for your plantings.

Add a decorative touch

Even simple touches can make a planter more attractive. Once you have the box assembled, draw or scribe lines on the sides, using a layout square to keep them parallel to the edges of the box. Set your circular saw to a depth of about one-third the thickness of the sides and cut grooves along the lines. Use a guide board or rip fence if necessary. Widen the grooves by making multiple offset passes with the saw.

Offset planked siding and add a cap

1 Attach the siding

Decking makes good siding for planters. Fasten planters to corner posts and add a 2×6 cleat at the bottom. The cleat acts as a stop for the shelf. Cut decking for the shelf.

Corner post

Shelf for container

2 Reinforce the cap

A cap will improve the appearance of the planter. Cut it from decking and miter the corners. Fasten L-brackets to hold the corners together, then use finishing nails to fasten the cap to the sides.

Place L-brackets inside perimeter of the sides.

Framing square

Small plants, small planter

Railings are just as good a spot for planters as any (but don't block your views). Use 1× or 5/4 stock of the same species used elsewhere in your deck and build the box wide enough to fit over the cap rail. These little units are also good for lining the edges of openings in the deck.

5/4×6 cap rail

Mitered corner

Offset 5/4×6 decking

Gap for circulation

PUT YOUR PLANTS ON WHEELS

Make your container garden a movable feast for the eyes by putting some of your planters on wheels.

Design the planter so the sides extend below the bottom of the corner posts by the height of the wheel (use small swivel casters) minus ¼ inch (so the box won't drag on the deck).

Assemble the planter, turn it upside down, and mark the centers of the corner posts. Drill holes in the center for the caster ferrule (what the caster swivels in). Drive the ferrule in and tap in the stem of the caster.

Constructing deck seating

- **TIME:** From 6 to 8 hours for a 5-foot bench, depending on the design and length
- **SKILLS:** Measuring, cutting, driving fasteners
- **TOOLS:** Tape measure, circular saw, cordless drill/driver, socket wrench, square, screwdriver, hammer, sander

Deck seating is more than just a place to sit down. Seating can define the perimeter of your deck and suggest different areas of use on it.

A well-designed built-in bench can contribute to the style of your deck almost as much as a well-designed railing—it's just shorter.

Benches should be between 15 and 18 inches high with seats at least 15 inches deep. For comfortable lounging, seats can be up to 30 inches deep. Build your benches from the same lumber as your railings so they won't look like an afterthought.

CAUTION

DON'T SUBSTITUTE SEATS FOR RAILINGS

Backless built-in perimeter seating is not a substitute for railings. If you build a 15-inch bench on a deck for which codes require a railing, building inspectors will probably insist you add a railing. Children will stand on benches, so railings behind benches need to be higher to provide adequate protection. Build a back on the bench when you need a railing too.

2×10 leg

Machine bolts (third bolt at bottom of leg not visible)

Seat rail

Cleat gives decking a nailing surface.

Perpendicular to joists

Mark the joists for the 2×10 legs, placing them the same distance from the header. Cut the legs and fasten them with three machine bolts in predrilled holes. Insert vertical blocking between the joists to keep the bench from rocking side to side.

Cut seat rails to match the depth of the bench seat and screw them to the legs. Add cleats to the outside of the legs so the decking cutout will have a nailing surface beneath it.

Cleats provide nailing surface for decking.

2×10 leg

Parallel to joists

Mark the joists to space the 2×10 legs at about half the length of the seat. Machine-bolt the legs to the joists and block the joists to keep the seat from rocking. Cut the seat rails to about 16 inches for a 19-inch bench seat and screw them to

the legs. Cleat both sides of the legs to give the decking a nailing surface. You can install the seat slats before or after finishing the decking, but if you do the slats first, you may bump your head when you attach the deck.

Perimeter bench

1 Make the legs

2×6 seat rail

22½° miter

Notched 4×6 post 15" to 17" long plus joist depth

Seat rail

2×6 front support

Cut the front 4×6 post and the 2×6 support 15 to 17 inches long plus the depth of the joist. Clamp the boards to the outer joists and drill carriage-bolt holes. Fasten the seat rails to the supports with lag screws.

2 Fasten the slats

2× seat slats

Overhang gauge

Cut seat slats to overhang the rails by 1 to 3 inches. Use 2×2 slats, as shown, or 2×3s ripped from wider stock. Set up an overhang gauge as shown above and at right and drive one fastener through each end of the slats.

Overhang gauge

½" plywood spacer

2×6 seat rail

Overhang gauge

2×2

For a 1½-inch overhang, clamp a 2×2 to the seat rails. Line up the slat ends flush with the outer face of the gauge and screw them to the rails, spacing them with a plywood spacer. Square the slats to the rails and attach them at the other ends the same way.

Butcher-block bench

Laminate a butcher-block bench

Cut each piece of the bench to length before assembling. Build it with a full-length slat and short leg on the outside and a short slat and full-height leg next, as shown. Align each slat carefully, flush at the top, then mark their positions and laminate them with screws and glue. Stagger the screws to avoid splitting the wood. Finish the bench to match the deck.

Attaching seats to railings

- **TIME:** Up to a full day to construct one section
- **SKILLS:** Measuring, cutting, fastening
- **TOOLS:** Circular saw, drill/driver, hammer, sander, socket wrench, square

Built-in deck perimeter seating must be designed to carry a heavy load, and nothing can provide better support than the railing posts. A perimeter bench is easy to build and because the railing posts support it, it doesn't require much extra lumber.

If possible posts should be located no more than 4 feet apart for proper support. Support bench spans wider than that with a 2×4 rail centered on the span and supported by short legs cut from 4×4s. This kind of seating can line the entire perimeter of the deck.

4×4 railing post

4×4 front post, 15½" (toenail to deck or use post base and trim)

Back support (optional) cut from 4×4 post

2×6 rail, 24" long

³⁄₈" carriage bolts

1 Make the plan

Build your bench from the same stock as your railing, using the dimensions shown above. Be sure modifications to this design do not reduce the strength of the bench.

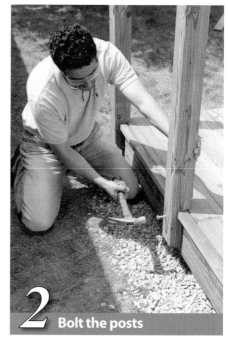

2 Bolt the posts

Cut bench posts to the same dimensions as your railing posts, predrilling them for carriage bolts and notching either the decking or the post, consistent with the railing posts.

3 Fasten seat rails

Using a framing square, mark the location of the front post. Cut the post from 4×4 stock and toenail it to the decking or fasten it with a post base (trim the base later). Clamp the seat rails to both posts, drill them, and fasten with carriage bolts.

4 Fasten the slats

Cut seat slats to length from 2×2, 2×3, or 2×4 stock, allowing at least a 1½-inch overhang. Fasten the slats to the rails with one or two fasteners at each end, depending on the slat width. Space the slats with pieces of ½-inch plywood.

5 Fasten the cap rail

Cut and install the back slats the same way. Then cut and fasten the 2×6 cap rail, mitering the corners. Sand the surfaces of the cap rail smooth and finish the bench to match the railing and deck.

Building privacy screens

■ **TIME:** About 3 hours per
6-foot bay, after setting posts
■ **SKILLS:** Measuring, squaring, plumbing,
cutting, fastening
■ **TOOLS:** Handsaw or circular saw,
hammer, screwdriver or cordless drill,
level, square, tape measure

Lattice is ideal for screening and for moderate privacy. Some deck sites, however, need more privacy than lattice can provide. The more privacy you need, the more solid the screen needs to be. Board-and-slat infill, louvers, and solid boards will close off the view but let some of the breeze flow through. You can build these structures as railing infill or fences if the screen needs to be placed off the deck itself.

SUPPORT THE SCREEN

The screens on this page are adaptations of popular fences. Their functions are similar—almost all fence designs can be built as railing infill. A small screen can be supported by posts bolted to the deck framing. A large screen should be connected to posts anchored to footings, especially if the screen will have to withstand heavy winds. Instead of building a screen onto a deck, consider installing a screen or a fence some distance away from the deck (see page 12).

Boards and slats

Board-and-slat infill, in either a fence or a railing, will increase your privacy and will add a little variety to the design of a solid board fence.

This design tends to look better with 1×4 boards and 1×2 slats. Make a spacer to hang on the rails to keep the spacing uniform throughout the panel.

Solid boards

A solid board fence offers maximum privacy, but carefully consider whether building one around your deck will make you feel walled in. This type of fence is better when placed farther from the deck site. Or place isolated solid panels at strategic points on the railing to provide almost complete privacy. They will add architectural contrast to other elements in the deck.

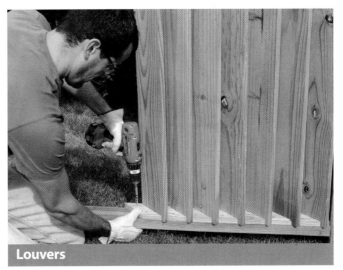

Louvers

Louvered screens (or fences) offer some of the same benefits as latticed screens, but they adapt to different landscape styles better. Louvers partially block the view and let in cooling breezes. They're also an effective design element in a setting that needs strong vertical lines.

Angled at 45 degrees 1×6 louvers are too wide for frames built with 4×4s, 2×4s, and 1×4s. You can rip them to fit, install them at a flatter angle, or build framing with nominal 6-inch lumber.

Framing a lattice screen

- **TIME:** About 1 hour per sheet after the frame is built
- **SKILLS:** Measuring, cutting lattice and trim
- **TOOLS:** Handsaw or circular saw, hammer, drill/driver, square, tape measure, level, chalkline

Lattice is popular screening material, suitable for both overheads and privacy screens. Usually sold in 4×8-, 2×8-, and 4×6-foot sheets, it's decorative and easy to install. Standard panels are ½ inch thick, but use ¾-inch lattice—it's tougher and will last longer, with almost no maintenance. The size of the spacing also varies. Plastic lattice panels that look similar to painted wood are also available.

Lattice can be easily framed between 1× stops attached to posts and rails. For a more finished appearance, trim the panels with milled moldings (below).

1 Make the frame

Plumb and fasten the posts to the rim joists or header (page 98) and attach rails. Mark the top and bottom of the posts inside the bays ¾ inch from the edge and snap a chalkline between the marks. Mark the inside edges of rails the same way. Finish-nail 1× stops at this line.

2 Fasten the lattice

Brush sealer on the edges of the lattice and paint or stain the panels before you hang them. Cut the panels to fit the bays and set them against the stops. Hold the lattice in place and install 1× stops with finishing nails. Do not drive fasteners into the lattice—only into the posts and rails.

Framing options

Dress up the frame

Details make a lot of difference in panel construction. Miter the corners of stops. You can top the posts with decorative caps or add a cap rail to the top.

Use milled stock

Stops for lattice can take many forms. If you want to dress up the looks of your lattice frame, attach quarter-round molding or rounded milled stock to the edges. Always make sure you drive the finishing nails into the posts and rails and not into the lattice. Seal or finish the milled stock before you install it.

Installing skirting

■ **TIME:** 8 to 10 hours to install about 40 feet of lattice

■ **SKILLS:** Creating a plan, measuring, cutting, fastening

■ **TOOLS:** Tape measure, drill/driver, hammer, circular saw, handsaw, framing square, layout square

Open space under a raised deck can mar the looks of even the most well-designed structure. Short shrubs at the rear of a colorful planting bed will hide the empty space and provide a pleasant transition from the deck to the yard. Lattice frames are another easily installed screen.

In a damp climate skirting will need to provide enough ventilation to prevent moisture problems. In dry climates ventilation isn't a primary need. If you make your skirting from 1× lumber instead of lattice, space the boards at ½-inch intervals. Wider spacing can make the pattern more interesting. You can use vinyl lattice if low (or no) maintenance is important to you—the plastic won't rot and needs no painting.

Provide a nailing surface for lattice with nailers inside the posts and along the bottom edge and fasten framed sections to the nailers. That way they will not cave in if you bump them with the lawn mower. If you want to use the space under a deck for storage, frame the sections so you can remove and reattach them.

Install a permanent skirt

1 Attach a nailing surface

Cut pressure-treated 2×2s or 2×4s to fit between the posts and toenail them at the top and bottom of the opening. Fasten the bottom nailer from 2 to 3 inches above the ground. Recess the nailers from the front edges of the posts if you want a reveal around the edges.

If the open space is 2 feet long or less, you probably won't need vertical supports, but in larger openings fasten vertical 2×s also. This provides a solid base for the lattice panel. Cut and install all the 2× framing before installing the lattice.

2 Fasten the lattice

Using the same kind of wood as you used in the railings, cut lattice panels to fit the openings and seal, stain, or paint all of the surfaces to protect them from the elements. Either frame the panels first, driving short screws from the rear of the lattice into 1×4 mitered frames, or screw the lattice panels to the 2× nailers and fasten the trim to the top.

121

Installing skirting *(continued)*

Install a removable skirt

1 Assemble the track

Removable lattice will need both solid support around its edges and a track that will allow you to remove it. Cut a pressure-treated 4×4 bottom rail to fit between the posts and fasten 1× stops along both of its top edges. This will leave a 2-inch open track in the center of the rail.

2 Set the bottom rail

Set the 4×4 bottom rail between the posts and attach it to the posts with brackets or toenailed fasteners. If the horizontal span is more than 3 feet, drill the rail and drive timber spikes into the ground at 2-foot intervals.

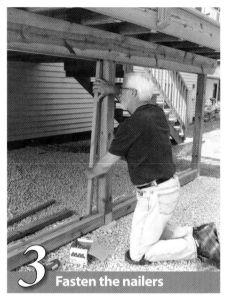

3 Fasten the nailers

In openings 6 feet or longer, cut 2×4 or 4×4 vertical supports and toenail them to the bottom rail and joist in the center of the opening. Cut 1× stops to fit the top and sides of each space and nail them to the posts, joists, and vertical supports, 2¾ inches back from the front of the posts.

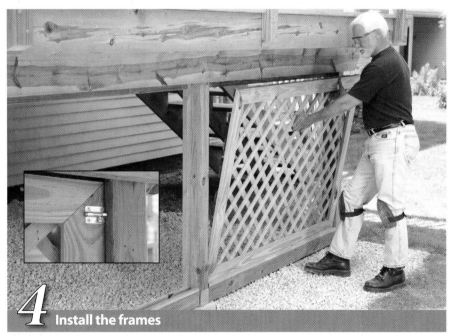

4 Install the frames

Cut lattice to fit the openings (less ⅛ inch all around) and prefinish it. Frame the lattice with 1×4 trim, mitering the corners. Drop the bottom edge of the frame into the track on the bottom rail. Install sliding-bolt locks in the corners of the panels (inset). Slide the locks open and lift the panel out to gain access to the space under the deck.

Install a solid skirt

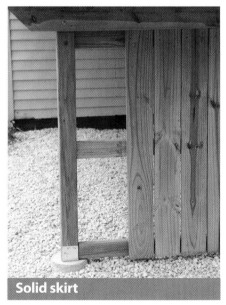

Solid skirt

For solid skirting use the techniques on this page to cut and fasten nailing surfaces for the boards. Use plywood siding, tongue-and-groove boards, or any other siding of your choice, fastening it to the nailing surfaces.

Building overhead structures

Support for an overhead structure on a deck depends on the size of the overhead and its location on the deck. The two corner posts of the deck can support a basic shade structure on one end of a deck. A pergola over a small deck could also be supported on the corner posts.

These examples require through posts, which are anchored in footings and extend past the deck to the top of the structure. You can attach through posts to the inside or outside of joists, depending on the design (page 102).

To simplify construction use a single-post corner (page 102) instead of a double-post design. A four-post overhead needs at least two posts supported by the decking and the framing under it.

Use beam and joist span tables (see page 44) when computing spans. That way you won't have to worry about the ceiling sagging under its own weight.

Rafter or seismic tie

Rafter

Beam

Post

Attach posts to deck joists or set on footings.

Build a freestanding overhead

Overheads can be freestanding or attached to the house. At a minimum freestanding overheads need support at their corners—posts set in a solid base (a footing or tied securely to the deck frame). If you're retrofitting an existing deck with an overhead, you'll have to either take up some of the deck to get at the framing or provide perimeter support with new posts anchored in footings.

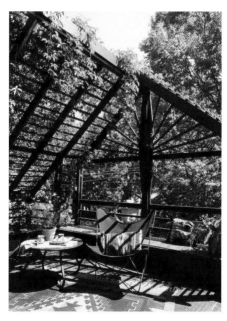

Simply for looks

An overhead usually provides shade. This one supports vines for shade on one side and lets sunlight onto the deck on the other.

Rafter

Flashing

Ledger attached to house

Beam

Post/beam connector

Seismic/ hurricane tie

Post

Attach posts to deck joists or set on footings.

Attach an overhead to the house

Overheads can be supported in part by a ledger attached to the house (see pages 52–57 for ledger installation). Add a beam supported by posts fastened to the deck joists or set on post footings. Attach the rafters to the beam with seismic ties to give the structure more stability.

Building overhead structures *(continued)*

BRACING POSTS

It's not easy to tell when to brace posts supporting an overhead structure. Local codes may not offer definitive answers. If your overhead is lightweight (loosely spaced slats, for example) and if one side is connected to a ledger at the house, you probably won't need bracing. On the other hand for a top-heavy overhead on a freestanding deck, assume that you should brace the posts. For everything in between build without bracing and check the stability of the structure before deciding. For guidance on bracing see page 82.

BRACING POSTS ON THE DECK SURFACE

Overhead posts centered between the joists need bracing. Cut a 4×4 to fit between the joists and lag-screw it in place, flush with the top of the joists. Screw 2×4 cleats to the joists on both sides of the 4×4. After you've laid the decking, drill through the deck and 4×4 brace, insert a bolt, and fasten the post anchor.

2×2 slats

2×6 rafter

2×8 beam

4×4 post

Vary this basic design to suit your deck

This overhead is easy to build and can be adjusted easily to provide the degree of shading you want. Double 2×8 beams span posts but could extend from a ledger. The 2×6 rafters set 16 inches on center can safely traverse spans up to 12 feet. Use rafter ties or 10d nails (through both sides) to fasten rafters to beams. Note that beam and rafter ends have matching tapers. (You can also use any of the other decorative cuts shown below.) Attach a top layer of 2×2 slats, spaced 4 to 8 inches apart; drive 8d nails through the slats into the rafters. Or use lattice for the top.

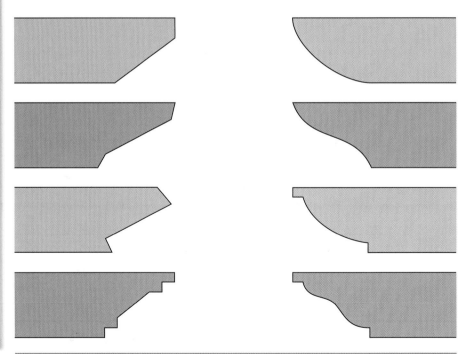

Choose a decorative rafter cut

One of the keys to making an attractive overhead structure is cutting dressed-up rafter ends. Find a decorative detail on the house or in the yard, then transfer it to the rafter ends. Make a template of plywood, hardboard, or cardboard, trace the design on each rafter, then cut.

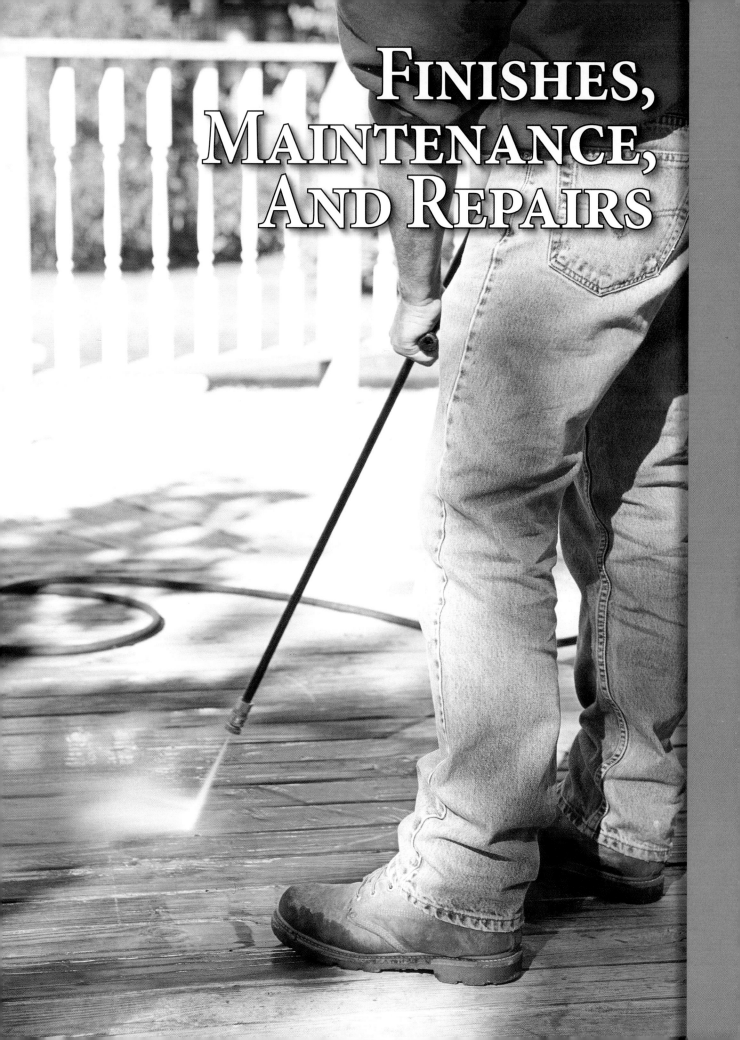

FINISHES, MAINTENANCE, AND REPAIRS

Selecting finishes

Even a well-built deck can't escape weathering. Unless you want the wood to weather into its natural gray tones, apply a protective coating. Coat the entire deck with a finish soon after you've completed it. Pressure-treated wood must be finished just like any other type of wood. It should be treated with a water repellent and regularly maintained with finishes that help keep the preservatives in the wood. Redwood and cedar also need protection, especially light-color sapwood.

Consider what finish to use before you build the deck, because the color will be a factor in your design. First consider color in a general way. Then turn your attention to possible shades of that color—dark brown, tan, pale red, or dark green.

Durability and ease of application are also important. Sealer is easiest to apply, followed by stain. Paint takes considerable time and effort.

Consider the wood too. A clear finish is a good choice for redwood and cedar because it allows their natural colors to show through. Treated lumber usually requires staining or painting to achieve the best appearance.

Sealer

Clear or lightly pigmented sealer protects the wood from water damage but doesn't change its color much. The best sealers contain additives that resist mildew formation, insect attacks, and fungus growth.

Ultraviolet (UV) blocking is a must to reduce damage caused by the sun's rays. Pigmented sealer offers all of the above protection; the pigment is put in to change the color of the wood slightly. Finally there is all-purpose sealer, which contains water repellent, preservative, and UV blocker.

You can apply sealer over or under stain and under primer and paint.

Stain

Unlike sealer the primary purpose of stain is to change the appearance of the wood. Some stains do so dramatically, others make more subtle changes. Certain formulas offer some protection to the wood, but if you want a full color change and full protection, then seal the wood and stain it (or vice versa depending on what you use).

The type of stain you use will depend on how much of the original wood tones you want left after its application. Semitransparent stain allows more wood grain to show through but wears away more quickly; it is particularly suitable for highlighting wood grain. Heavy-bodied stain contains more pigment and hides the grain. Some heavy-bodied formulations are almost like paint.

All stains—whether oil- or water-base, including those not designed to penetrate the fibers of the wood—tend to retain the wood's natural look far better than paint.

Paint

Paint conceals some defects, can last a long time, and can look great in certain designs. Exterior alkyds are more costly, more difficult to clean up, and slower drying. They can also wear well, which will reduce the need to repaint. Latex paint costs less, cleans up easily, and dries quickly but may not wear well on deck surfaces.

WATCH YOUR VOCS

Wood finishes of all kinds have undergone drastic changes in recent years. In an effort to clean up the air, many states have passed legislation requiring manufacturers to reduce the volatile organic compounds (VOCs) in their finishes.

VOCs evaporate as the finish cures. VOCs from wood finishes, especially from solvent-base (oil-base) finishes, are considered pollutants; low-VOC finishes are available. Latex paint or stain and other water-base finishes have been less affected by the regulations since water is the principal evaporator. Some (but not all) of these new products generally do not last as long as oil-base finishes.

INGREDIENTS IN DECK FINISHES

Ingredient	Description	Uses	Comments
Water repellent	Wax, usually paraffin, suspended in a binder	Prevents water from soaking into the wood	Very easy to apply but requires annual or biannual applications
Preservative	Typically includes a mildew retardant, sometimes an insecticide	Prevents fungi, especially mildew, from growing on the wood; repels insects such as termites	Should be used regularly on most decks in most parts of the country
UV stabilizer	Reduces degradation of wood due to ultraviolet radiation	Frequently added to clear finishes	Not usually as effective as pigment in preventing damage
Pigment	One or more ingredients that give color to the finish	Found in paint, solid-color stain, and semitransparent stain	Protects very well against UV and water damage but ages quickly on decks

When to apply sealer

How can you tell if your deck needs sealing? Sometimes the answer is obvious. Old wood that looks dried out needs sealer. But looks can be deceiving; boards that look brand-new and freshly stained or sealed may also be in danger of drying out.

Perform a quick test once or twice a year. Sprinkle a little water on the surface.

If the water beads up and does not soak in within two minutes, the deck is sealed well enough. If water soaks in within two minutes, it's time to apply sealer.

Just to make sure try the test in several places on your deck. You may find shaded areas are just fine, but spots that are not protected from the sun may need a selective application.

USE PRODUCTS WITH HIGH-QUALITY INGREDIENTS

Select the ingredients you want in your finish from the chart on page 126, then look for a product that lists them. A better, more-expensive finish has solvents, repellents, preservatives, and pigments that soak deep into the wood. It will last longer than less-expensive products that don't get much below the surface. A paint dealer or deck specialist can tell you which products are the most durable. These will cost more per application—not only more per gallon—because the deck will soak up more. However they will save you time and money in the long run because they need to be applied less often.

Film-forming finishes

Film-forming finishes—paint, lacquer, and varnish—create a solid film on the surface of the wood but with mixed results. Lacquer isn't suitable for decks at all. It isn't tough enough to stand up to weather and wear. Most varnish can't take the sun, although modern high-quality water-base polyurethane finishes may hold up on sites where exposure is limited.

New, unpainted surfaces should be primed first. Oil-base primer provides better protection on raw wood than water-base primer. Add a stain blocker to stop bleed-through from redwood and cedar. A good-quality acrylic-latex top coat applied over an alkyd primer makes a durable finish.

Staining pressure-treated lumber

Fresh off the rack pressure-treated lumber has a yellow-green or reddish brown cast. Left alone on your deck, it weathers to a gray you might find unattractive. That doesn't mean you have to live with this color.

Let the wood dry for a couple of weeks, then try the water bead test ("When to apply sealer, "page 127). Apply a coat or two of stain and the deck will look like it's redwood or cedar. You'll have to reapply every year or two to maintain that look.

GETTING THE LOOK YOU WANT

The Wet Look: For a long-lasting glossy finish that makes your deck always look like it has just rained, buy an alkyd resin enamel or varnish that is made for the type of wood and conditions you have. (Some do not work well if the deck will stay wet for long periods.) Follow the manufacturer's instructions.

As Close as Possible to the Wood's Original Look: Apply a transparent stain containing a UV (ultraviolet) inhibitor or blocker. The finish will contain some pigment (there's no other way to block out the effects of the sun), so it will change the color of the wood slightly. If you don't use a stain with UV protection, the sun will change your wood's color more dramatically.

Silvery Gray: If you have high-quality redwood or cedar, composed entirely of dark-color heartwood (instead of cream-color sapwood), you may not need any finish. The wood will turn a soft, shiny gray. But the wood may crack and splinter because it's not protected from wet-dry cycles. A clear finish containing water repellent will allow the color to change without cracking. If you let pressure-treated lumber go untreated, it will turn a dirty gray, not silvery.

Removing the Gray: If your deck has already turned gray and you want to change it, wash it with wood bleach. This will not restore the original color of the wood, but it will give you a bleached wood that can be stained to the color of your choice. Commercial deck restorers—usually bleaches—are available.

DON'T WAIT

You might be told that a deck should dry out for months before applying a finish. Don't believe it. The most important coat of finish your deck receives will be the first one.

On a new deck built with pressure-treated lumber, let the deck dry out two to four weeks, depending on weather conditions.

Untreated lumber should be finished as soon as it is dry to the touch. If you wait too long, the surface of the wood may already have begun to degrade.

Oil-base clear sealer

Thin and easily applied oil-base sealer flows readily and soaks into the wood quickly. You may need more than one application on new wood.

Water-base clear sealer

Latex sealer can be applied quickly and cleanup is easy. The water base makes the product low in VOCs (see page 126) and safer to use.

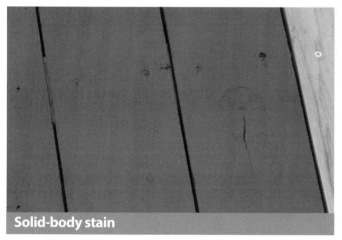

Solid-body stain

Heavy pigment will change the color of the wood completely and hide much of the grain pattern. The opaque stain creates a solid tone across the surface of the deck.

Semitransparent stain

This finish is an effective compromise: It alters the wood tone somewhat but leaves much of the grain pattern exposed.

Paint

Apply paint if you want an opaque finish. The best paint bonds to the surface but doesn't soak in. Choose epoxy or oil-base paint for a long life.

SAMPLE IN A CORNER

Before applying any deck finish—stain or paint especially—know how the final color will look. The only way to really be sure is to see the color when the finish is dry.

Test the final color by applying a small amount in an out-of-the-way spot on your deck or on a scrap of the same kind of decking. Let the finish dry to make sure it produces the color you want. Paints usually are darker when they dry. Stains dry lighter.

Applying deck finishes

- **TIME:** About 4 hours for an average deck
- **SKILLS:** No special skills, just read and follow instructions
- **TOOLS:** Sanding pole, brush; optional application tools include sprayer, roller, or pad

Home centers have a wide variety of deck cleaners, sealers, and finishes. Check with deck owners in your area to see which products work best. Decks exposed to hot sun for long periods may need a coat of sealer every year.

A deck that has turned gray can usually be made to look like new if you clean it and apply a finish.

Manufacturers of paints, stains, and repellents change or adjust ingredients in their finishes, so application instructions might change as well. Always read the label and follow instructions carefully. Many companies have toll-free numbers to call for technical questions. Your local supplier can advise you on which product to use and how to get the best results from the finish.

For best results clean and lightly sand the deck before applying a finish. Wait for a dry but slightly overcast day—too much sun will set the finish before it has a chance to soak into the wood.

You may want to hire a professional to finish or refinish your deck. Look through your phone book for companies that restore, finish, and maintain decks. Get estimates and examine some of the decks they have worked on. Compare the cost with the time and expense it will take you to do it yourself.

WHEN TO RECOAT

Recoat water-repellent deck finishes at least once a year. Semitransparent stain should be recoated every two to three years. But these are general rules; decks in different locations that are treated with different finishes may require very different refinishing schedules. You can tell when a semitransparent stain has begun to age by comparing how much color has worn away. Compare the tone of the finish in an exposed spot with one that doesn't see much sun or get much use. A noticeable difference means you should recoat.

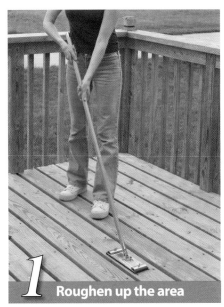

1 Roughen up the area

Before applying finish on a new deck, go over the wood with 80- or 100-grit sandpaper to roughen the surface and encourage absorption. Use a sanding pole to speed up the sanding and prevent a backache.

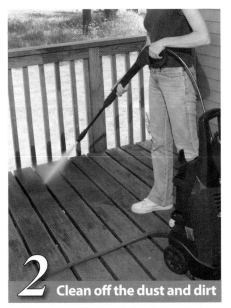

2 Clean off the dust and dirt

A clean deck will absorb finish better than a dirty one. Sweep thoroughly, rinse with a hose or power washer, and let the deck dry. If your deck is already showing signs of age, scrub it with a chlorine bleach solution or deck cleaner.

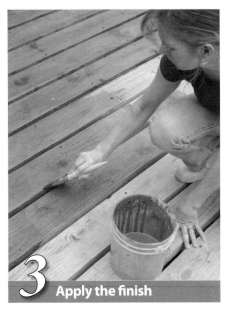

3 Apply the finish

To prevent lap marks maintain a wet edge—don't let the finish dry in an area before you overlap it with wet finish. This is particularly important with pigmented finishes. If you use a roller or sprayer, have someone right behind you with a brush to work the finish into the wood before it dries.

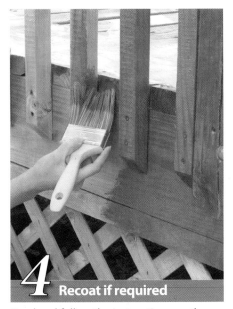

4 Recoat if required

Read and follow the instructions on the label. Some clear deck finishes require a second coat. Always apply an extra coat or two to any exposed end grain. Semitransparent stains often require only a single coat; additional coats may cause excessive color or leave visible brush marks.

Maintaining and troubleshooting decks

- **TIME:** An annual inspection should take 1 or 2 hours
- **SKILLS:** Diagnosing rotting wood and analyzing potential structural failures
- **TOOLS:** Hammer, flashlight, pry bar, circular saw, awl, screwdriver, putty knife

Good construction techniques, high-quality materials, and regular maintenance will add many years to the life of a deck. Yet even the most well-constructed deck has inherent weak spots:

- between the house and ledger
- where posts are connected
- boards with exposed end grain
- railing joints
- notched joints
- joints in the decking

By finding and repairing problems early, you can avoid expensive repairs later. Inspect your deck thoroughly at least once a year. If possible inspect beneath the deck surface. If your deck is too close to the ground for you to crawl under it, remove some decking boards to get a good look.

Look for soft spots, indicating rot. Poke the wood with a screwdriver. If parts of your deck seem to be in worse shape than others, try to find the source of the problem before attempting a repair. Perhaps water damage is occurring because of faulty gutters or the accumulation of leaves or dirt.

If you find potentially serious problems at the ledger, posts, beams, or joists, consult a professional. You can make most repairs yourself, but some are complicated projects.

Check the ledger

The connection between the deck and the house is particularly critical. Check that flashing is in good condition. Probe with an awl or screwdriver for water damage on the ledger. Check for fungi, blue or black stains, and little piles of sawdust indicating the presence of termites or carpenter ants. Tighten all fasteners.

Check the posts

Check posts most carefully at the ground line and at the top. Use a probe to inspect for rot by sticking it into various parts of the post and comparing the ease of penetration. Try to find out if there are soft spots inside the post, where rot often begins. Inspect and secure the post's connection with the foundation.

Check beneath the deck

Inspect beneath your deck. Put on old clothes and bring a flashlight and a screwdriver with you. Poke the undersides of decking boards, all around the ledger, posts, stringers, and treads, and in any other joints and crevices.

Look for the loose ones

Loose decking may not indicate a structural problem and may only require retightening the fasteners. Tighten the ones you can and mark the ones that need replacement. If the decking is damaged, remove it (page 136) and install new boards.

Maintaining and troubleshooting decks *(continued)*

Check the railings

Railings, and especially stair rails, often have to withstand extra strain. Inspect posts for damage and make sure all fasteners are secure and tight. Look at the ends of all rails for water damage. Replace damaged balusters.

Check the decking

Decking boards split at the ends will often continue to separate along their length. You can try cutting the boards flush with the joists and sealing the cut ends, but in most cases it's better to replace split boards with new ones. For internal cracks sand the surface and apply several coats of sealer.

Clutter will rot

Dirt, leaves, or other natural debris that collects between the decking or in other crevices can hold moisture for weeks. That can cause rot but is easily prevented with regular cleaning. Pressure-washing is an effective way to clean out crevices.

FOR PESTS GET A PRO

Termites and other wood-borers can feast on your deck. Pressure-treated lumber rated for ground contact should resist insect infestation, but redwood and cedar aren't guaranteed to be pest-free.

wood-eating insects like to eat in the dark, so they tunnel along the grain lines inside the wood. By the time you notice the damage, it's too late. If you see tunnels running inside a board or small piles of fine sawdust at the edge of a board, call a professional exterminator.

KEEP IT CLEAN

Because you see your deck change slowly, you might not notice when it's time to clean or refinish it. Make a calendar to help you stay ahead of the dirt and grime.

Little things can have big results. Sweeping and removing debris, for example, helps reduce trapped moisture and the chances of rot. Cleaning gives a drab deck a fresh, new look. You'll be surprised how much bigger a clean deck looks.

- Sweep the surface once a week—more often if the weather and usage require it.
- Scrub the deck with warm water and a mild detergent monthly.
- If simple washing does not get it clean enough, or if you want to lighten the color of the deck, buy a deck-cleaning product.

- If the wood is dirty and weathered, clean it with a solution of oxalic acid and water. Scrub an area with a stiff natural-bristle brush, rinse, allow to dry, and repeat if necessary. Wear protective clothing—oxalic acid is caustic.
- To clear away all the dirt at once—along with any debris, dirt stuck in joints, or loose paint—rent a power washer. Clean the deck with a fan-tip nozzle so you won't damage the surface with a 1,200 pounds-per-square-inch (psi) blast. Used improperly a high-pressure power washer can splinter and gouge the surface of lumber.

Removing mildew

If your wood is cedar, a spot of black slime may not be mildew—it could be a natural substance that sometimes leaches out. Just wash it off with a mild soap-and-water solution. If you have other types of wood or if the black slime persists and seems related to moisture, then it may be mildew. It won't affect the strength of your wood, but you should get rid of it.

Use a commercial deck cleaner or mix 1 part chlorine bleach to 3 parts water. Use a stiff brush to work the solution into the wood. Rinse thoroughly with clean water and let the deck dry. This solution can also restore some of the natural color to the deck. When you apply the next coat of finish to the deck, be sure it contains a mildew retardant.

Replace popped nails

As decking shrinks nailheads may need to be hammered in farther. Over time, however, nails may start loosening in their holes. In this case carefully remove the nails with a flat pry bar. Put a piece of scrap wood under the bar to keep from denting the surface of your deck. Replace the nails with 3-inch decking screws. Or drive new nails into the old holes in the decking but at a different angle.

AVOID CORROSION WITH STAINLESS STEEL

Steel fasteners used on decks are usually galvanized to prevent corrosion that could stain the surrounding wood. Over time most galvanized fasteners begin to corrode. Double-coated and anodized decking screws resist corrosion better than electroplated galvanized screws, but even they may lose their coatings eventually.

If you live in an area with particularly high humidity or where the deck may be exposed to salt water, corrosion will begin sooner. In these cases stainless-steel fasteners may be a bargain in the long run because they won't corrode. They look great too.

Maintaining and troubleshooting decks *(continued)*

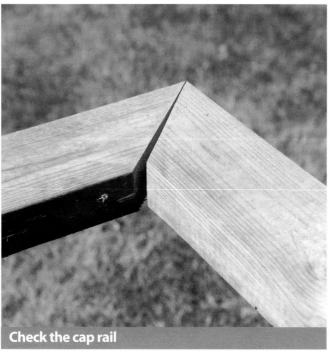

Check the cap rail

Cap rails, especially cantilevered ones, can separate at the seams. Usually you can't rejoin the existing pieces. Start with wood of the same species as the rest of your rail and replace one or both sides of the rail (page 135).

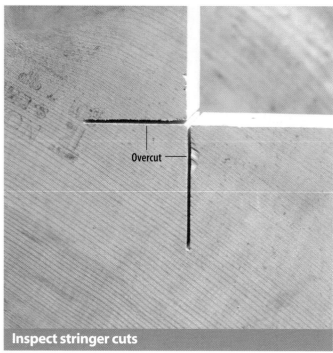

Overcut

Inspect stringer cuts

If you have a deck with stairs, pay attention to the stringers. Look underneath or pull off the treads and make sure the runs and rises are not overcut. If they are they'll collect water and may eventually break. Replace stringers that have overcuts.

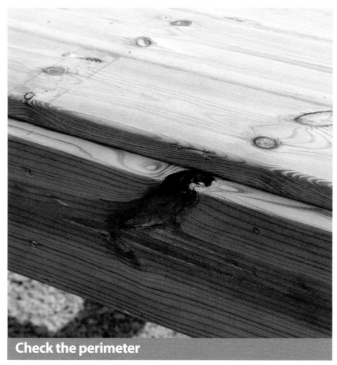

Check the perimeter

Moisture can get into the joint if a decking board is not flush with the framing and doesn't overhang it. If your deck has this fault, replace the last three or four boards, spacing them so the last board overhangs the framing.

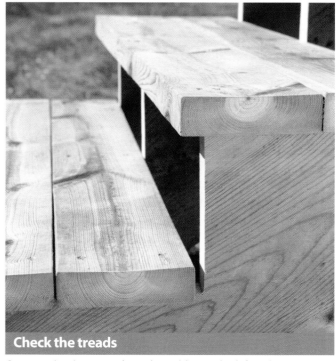

Check the treads

Overcuts (top) are not the only problem to look for when checking your stairs. Misaligned treads and treads less than 10 inches deep can also pose problems. Replace them with new material.

Repairing a deck

It's not unusual to find several damaged decking boards on a deck that's otherwise in good condition. Replacing a board or two is not difficult, and the replacements are more likely to stay attached if you refasten them with 3½- to 4-inch deck screws.

New boards, if they are of the same species as the old ones, will blend in with the color of the old boards after a year or two. But you don't have to wait that long to make all the boards look the same. If you clean and refinish the entire deck, the new and old wood will look almost alike.

Decking boards should have gaps about ⅛ inch wide between them so water can seep through the deck after a rainfall. If a gap is filled with debris, clean it out with a stiff broom. If that doesn't work use a putty knife. Widen gaps that have closed with a circular saw (but don't cut the joists).

If you find several framing members that are substantially rotten, consider tearing down the deck (see pages 137–138) and starting over. If the boards are not severely damaged or if you are certain that only a few are rotten, repairs may solve those problems. Consult a professional deck builder if you are not sure.

If a deck feels spongy when you jump on it, it may be underbuilt, with joists or beams that are too small for their spans (see page 44). If you have room to work underneath, you may be able to shore up a weak deck by installing a new beam with posts and footings. This is slow, tedious work. To add some extra strength, install a row of blocking at the middle of the joists (see page 74) and support it with a post or two.

Repair the cap rail

Use the old miter as a template for the new one.

1 Mark the new rail

If the cap rail is mostly in good condition, clean the joints with a putty knife and seal them. If a joint is rotten, remove the cap and use it to mark the angle for cutting new wood (of the same species).

Scrap holds new and old sections together.

2 Fasten the corners

Miter the replacement rail, then cut the other end to length. Snug both faces of the corner by clamping them with a scrap 2×4. Drill pilot holes and drive one 3-inch screw into each edge and two screws into each post.

Repair warped decking

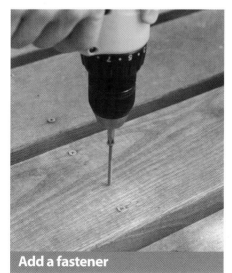

Add a fastener

An additional fastener will often bring a warped board into its proper place. Predrill the decking (but not the joist) and drive a screw next to the existing fasteners. Or remove the old fasteners and drive a new set of 3½-inch screws.

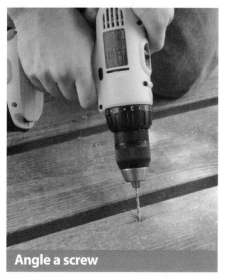

Angle a screw

An angled fastener has more holding power than one driven perpendicular to the decking. Clamp a warped board down and predrill it at an angle. Drive the screw. You may have to wait a week for the board to partially flatten, then drive in a longer screw to pull it down more.

Repairing a deck *(continued)*

Remove decking

1 Pry out the pop-ups

Pry out popped nails with a pry bar, inserting a wide putty knife under the heel of the bar to protect the decking if necessary (see Step 3).

2 Dig out the nails

A cat's paw will lift most stubborn nails but not without digging into the wood. If the board is going in the scrap pile, pry up the nail about ¼ inch with a cat's paw. Finish pulling it out with a framing hammer.

3 Remove the decking

Removing decking calls for caution; you don't want to dent neighboring boards. If possible start prying where the board overhangs the joist. If not use a pry bar and a wide putty knife to lift the damaged board out.

Remove stubborn screws

Increase your torque

Working away at a stubborn screw with your cordless screwdriver tip will strip out the head, and you won't have enough left for the bit to grip. Instead clamp a locking pliers near the tip of a screwdriver shaft. Put all your weight on the screwdriver and use the pliers to turn it.

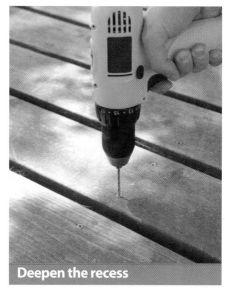

Deepen the recess

If a locking pliers won't get the screw out, drill a ⅛-inch hole into the center of a phillips head. Tap the screwdriver in the recess to create a new binding surface. Then try turning it again.

Cut the screw

If you can get under the board—where it overhangs the framing, for example, or by removing adjacent boards—cut the screw with a reciprocating saw equipped with a metal-cutting blade.

Removing an old deck

- **TIME:** 6 to 8 hours to tear down a 12×16-foot deck
- **SKILLS:** Rough cutting, lifting, prying
- **TOOLS:** Reciprocating saw, chalkline, circular saw, pry bar, hacksaw, drill/driver

Sometimes you just have to tear down an old deck. Perhaps the style or size of the old structure is simply not appropriate for your lifestyle or landscape design. Perhaps you are planning a major addition to your house—an extra bedroom, new family room, or bigger kitchen—and the old deck is in the way. Perhaps the construction of the old deck was shoddy, or previous owners did not maintain it and it's now almost falling down on its own.

Removing an old deck is not a difficult chore. Before you get out the reciprocating saw and order the roll-off trash bin, however, make sure that removing the deck is what you want to do.

If it's more outdoor space you want, you can build onto a sound existing deck in a number of ways. If you need more shade, you can add an arbor, an awning, or a pergola. If you just don't like the way the old deck looks, maybe a new railing or even new decking will save you the trouble of tearing it all down and rebuilding.

All of these options, of course, assume a deck whose structural integrity is sound. If the deck is simply too poorly built or too deteriorated to justify keeping it, then tear it down.

Like construction, demolition follows a logical, safe sequence. Take the deck down in steps, as shown on this page and the next. Work carefully.

If you're going to replace an old structure with a new one, think about how much of the existing material you want to salvage and recycle. You may be able to reuse structural lumber as well as other parts of the deck. But recycling is not without its consequences. You can pry up nailed lumber with a pry bar, but you're likely to split the wood beyond usefulness.

Screwed-down boards can't be pried without ruining them, and removing the thousand or so screws in a deck will take a long time. Nailed framing connectors can be pried up, but the connectors will probably bend. Removing screws from framing connectors will leave the connectors intact but may not be cost-efficient.

After considering all of that, you'll probably think it makes more sense to dismantle the deck with a reciprocating saw as shown here. Joists and decking that have been cut can still be used in the new deck if they're in good condition and long enough. You can recycle boards for blocking, bracing, planters, and seating.

Order a waste container and set it as close as possible to the site without ruining the lawn. Cut the pieces into lengths you—and a helper—can comfortably carry. Find out what your dumping fees will be—some municipalities charge more for pressure-treated lumber because they can't dispose of it by burning it.

If your old deck has a water feature or lighting of any kind, find the water supply and power lines. Turn the power and water off before you start. Wear gloves, safety glasses, and a dust mask. Old wood can release mold spores that can get into your lungs.

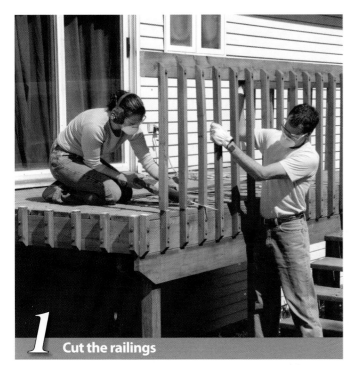

1 Cut the railings

Cut railings into sections. Using a reciprocating saw cut the top and bottom rails at the posts. Have someone hold the railing while you cut. Cut balusters across the decking if they are attached to the joists.

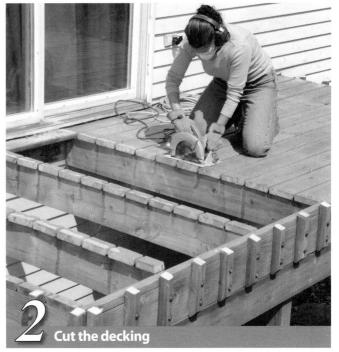

2 Cut the decking

Snap chalklines to indicate one side of each joist. Set your circular saw to the depth of the decking and cut the decking into sections. Remove stair treads by unscrewing or prying out the fasteners.

Removing an old deck *(continued)*

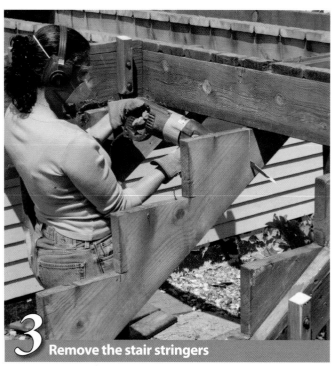

3 Remove the stair stringers

Holding your reciprocating saw so it will clear the joists, cut the tops of the stringers from the joists. Pry the stringers off the landing pad or the toe-kick.

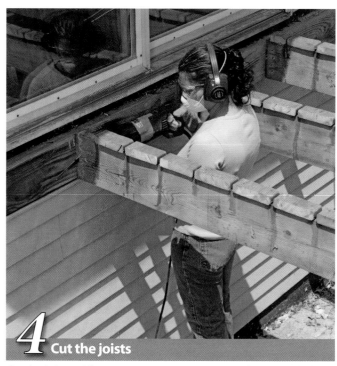

4 Cut the joists

Cut the joists with a reciprocating saw, sawing where the blade won't hit the joist hangers. Don't force the cut; let the weight of the saw set the pace.

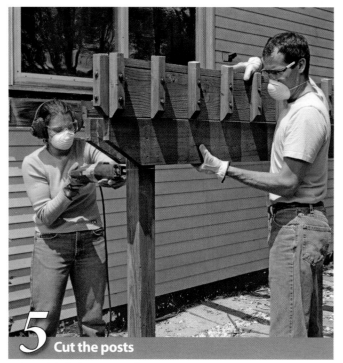

5 Cut the posts

Using a blade long enough to cut in one pass, cut the posts under the beam. Have someone help support the beam so it won't fall away when you complete the cut. Cut the posts off at the bottom, just above the anchor. Remove the anchor and saw the bolt off with a hacksaw.

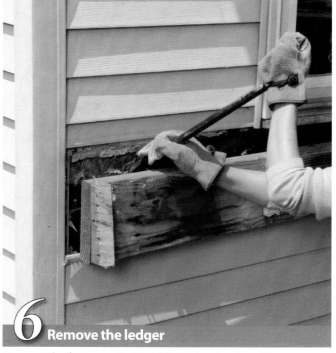

6 Remove the ledger

Unscrew the fasteners that hold the ledger in place. Have someone help you hold the ledger as you remove the fasteners so it won't fall off and hurt you. Pry the ledger off with a pry bar if necessary. Remove the flashing and repair or replace the siding if you aren't installing another ledger.

Glossary

For more information refer to the index on pages 141–143.

Actual dimension. The actual size of dimension lumber after milling and drying. See nominal dimension.

Anchor. Metal device set in concrete for attaching posts to footings or piers.

Backfill. To replace earth excavated during construction. A material other than the original earth may be used.

Baluster. A vertical railing member, usually spaced between posts.

Beam. A horizontal framing member that usually rests on posts and supports the joists.

Bevel cut. An angled cut through the thickness of a piece of wood.

Blocking. Short pieces of lumber between joists to keep the joists from twisting and to strengthen the framing.

Board. A piece of lumber that is less than 2 inches thick.

Board foot. One board foot is 1 square foot that is 1 inch thick; a piece that measures 1×12×12 inches.

Bracing. Crosspieces, often diagonal, nailed and bolted between tall posts, usually those more than 5 feet tall.

Broom finish. A slip-resistant texture made by brushing a stiff broom across freshly poured concrete.

Butt joint. The joint formed when two pieces of material meet end-to-end, end-to-face, or end-to-edge.

Cantilever. A member with a free end that extends beyond its support.

Chamfer. A partial bevel cut made along the end or edge of a board.

Check. A crack on the surface of a board. A check that runs more than halfway through the thickness of a board weakens the board.

Flashing. Strips of metal, usually galvanized steel or aluminum, used for weather protection.

Flush. On the same plane as, or level with, the surrounding surface.

Footing. A small foundation, usually made of concrete, that supports a post.

Frost heave. The movement of soil caused when soil moisture freezes. Posts and footings that do not extend below the frost line are subject to frost heave.

Frost line. The maximum depth to which the ground in an area freezes during winter.

Grain. The direction and pattern of fibers in a piece of wood.

Hardwood. Lumber that comes from deciduous trees (which lose their leaves).

Header. A framing member across the ends of the joists.

Heartwood. The center and most durable part of a tree.

Joist. Horizontal framing members that support a floor or ceiling.

Joist hanger. A metal connector used to join a joist to a ledger or header.

KDAT (kiln-dried after treatment). Lumber that has been dried after being treated with preservatives; more expensive than pressure-treated lumber but less likely to warp.

Kerf. The void created as the blade of a saw cuts through a piece of material.

Lag screw. A large screw with heavy threads and a hexagonal head that can be driven with a wrench or socket.

Lap joint. The joint formed when one member overlaps another.

Ledger. A horizontal board that supports framing members.

Level. The condition that exists when a surface is horizontal (parallel to the horizon). Also a tool used to determine level.

Load. Weights and forces that a structure is designed to withstand.

Miter joint. The joint formed when two members meet that have been cut at the same angle (usually 45 degrees).

Molding. Wood that covers exposed edges or serves as decoration.

Nominal dimension. The stated size of a piece of lumber, such as a 2×4 or a 1×12. Actual dimensions are smaller.

On center (OC). The distance from the center of one regularly spaced member to the center of the next.

Pergola. An open overhead structure designed to provide shade.

Pier. Concrete, usually preformed in a pyramidal shape, used to support a post.

Pilot hole. A hole to prevent splitting the wood when driving a screw or nail.

Plan view. A drawing that shows an overhead view of a deck.

Plumb. The condition that exists when a member is at true vertical, pointing to the earth's center of gravity.

Plywood. A building material made of sheets of wood veneer laminated with their grain at 90 degrees to each other.

Post. A vertical framing piece that supports a beam or a joist.

Pressure-treated (PT) wood. Lumber and sheet materials impregnated with a chemical solution to resist rot.

Rabbet. A step-shaped cut made along the edge of a piece of wood.

Rail. A horizontal framing member that spans between posts to support balusters and sometimes the cap rail.

Glossary *(continued)*

Ready-mix concrete. Wet concrete delivered by truck ready to pour.

Rim joist. A joist at the outside edge of a framing layout.

Rip cut. A cut made parallel to the length of a board or its grain to reduce the board's width.

Rise. Total rise is the vertical distance a stairway climbs. Unit rise is the vertical distance between the surfaces of two consecutive treads.

Riser. A board attached to the vertical cut surface of a stair stringer used to cover the gap between treads and to provide additional tread support.

Run. Total run is the total horizontal distance a stairway spans from the structure to grade. Unit run is the horizontal depth of a tread cut made in a stringer.

Sapwood. The lighter-color recent growth of any species of wood.

Sealer. A protective coating (usually clear) applied to wood or metal.

Set a nail. To drive the head of a nail slightly below the surface of the wood.

Setback. The minimum distance between a property line and any structure, as specified by local building and zoning rules.

Shim. A thin strip or wedge of wood or other material used to fill a gap between two adjoining components or to help establish level or plumb.

Site plan. A map of a property that shows major permanent features, such as the house, outbuildings, and trees.

Skirt or skirting. Pieces of lumber installed around the perimeter of a deck to conceal the area below the decking. Skirting may be made of solid boards, either vertical or horizontal, or of lattice, to allow for air movement.

Sleeper. Horizontal wood member laid directly on the ground, a patio, or a roof to support decking.

Softwood. Lumber derived from evergreen trees (which don't lose their leaves).

Span. The distance traveled by a beam, joist, or decking board between supporting structures.

Square. The condition that exists when one surface is at a 90-degree angle to another. Also a tool used to determine square.

Stringer. A sloping board used to support treads and risers on a stairway. Stringers are usually made of 2×12s.

Toenail. To drive a nail at an angle to hold together two pieces of material.

Tongue-and-groove. A joint made using boards that have a projecting tongue on one edge and a matching groove on the opposite edge.

Wane. The rounded-off corner along the edge of a board, where there once was bark.

Warp. Any of several lumber defects caused by uneven shrinkage of wood cells during drying.

Index

Index (continued)

METRIC CONVERSIONS

U.S. Units to Metric Equivalents			Metric Units to U.S. Equivalents		
To convert from	**Multiply by**	**To get**	**To convert from**	**Multiply by**	**To get**
Inches	25.4	Millimeters	Millimeters	0.0394	Inches
Inches	2.54	Centimeters	Centimeters	0.3937	Inches
Feet	30.48	Centimeters	Centimeters	0.0328	Feet
Feet	0.3048	Meters	Meters	3.2808	Feet
Yards	0.9144	Meters	Meters	1.0936	Yards
Miles	1.6093	Kilometers	Kilometers	0.6214	Miles
Square inches	6.4516	Square centimeters	Square centimeters	0.1550	Square inches
Square feet	0.0929	Square meters	Square meters	10.764	Square feet
Square yards	0.8361	Square meters	Square meters	1.1960	Square yards
Acres	0.4047	Hectares	Hectares	2.4711	Acres
Square miles	2.5899	Square kilometers	Square kilometers	0.3861	Square miles
Cubic inches	16.387	Cubic centimeters	Cubic centimeters	0.0610	Cubic inches
Cubic feet	0.0283	Cubic meters	Cubic meters	35.315	Cubic feet
Cubic feet	28.316	Liters	Liters	0.0353	Cubic feet
Cubic yards	0.7646	Cubic meters	Cubic meters	1.308	Cubic yards
Cubic yards	764.55	Liters	Liters	0.0013	Cubic yards

To convert from degrees Fahrenheit (F) to degrees Celsius (C), first subtract 32, then multiply by ⁵/₉.

To convert from degrees Celsius to degrees Fahrenheit, multiply by ⁹/₅, then add 32.

Dream it. Build it.

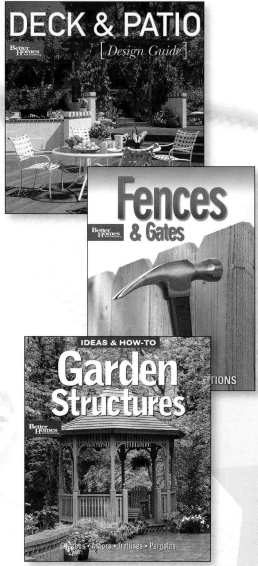

DECK & PATIO *[Design Guide]*

Fences & Gates

IDEAS & HOW-TO Garden Structures

Gazebos • Arbors • Trellises • Pergolas

Imagine living in a space customized for you, by you. These great titles will help your dreams come true with **advice + inspiration + ideas + step-by-step how-to** for designing, building, and maintaining your home projects.